DIVIDED SOCIETY

PAPERS OF THE 1991
ANNUAL GENERAL MEETING
OF THE
NATIONAL CONFERENCE
OF PRIESTS OF IRELAND

RYAN REPORT ON
RENEWAL COURSES FOR PRIESTS

DOMINICAN PUBLICATIONS

First published (1992) by
Dominican Publications
42 Parnell Square
Dublin 1

ISBN 1-871552-25-7

Printed in Ireland at
Colour Books Ltd
Baldoyle
Dublin 13

Contents

Introduction

Harry Bohan

It is now fifteen years since NCPI met for the first time. Even in that short space of time, there have been many major changes in the world and in the Church. Many of these changes have had an influence on the life and ministry of priests. At a local level, at the level of parish, our lives vary in terms of demands and commitments. Most of us have discovered that effective time and people management is difficult to achieve. Some of us look back and have tried to recall the 'good old days' when our influence was far greater than it is today.

Those recollections could be summed up in the story linked with Cardinal Cullen who told the assembled bishops at the First Vatican Council that the ordinary people of Ireland believed in the infallibility of the pope. An American bishop quipped: 'The ordinary people of Ireland believe that their parish priest is infallible!' I think we would acknowledge that the importance of the parish priest has declined greatly in the intervening years. Vatican II set out and outlined the dignity of the bishops as successors of the apostles on the one hand and on the other the important role of the laity, the People of God. An Irish parish priest was heard to exclaim after Vatican II: 'When this Council is over, the

1

bishop will have all the power, the laity will have all the glory, the priest will have all the work!'

It will probably take a third Vatican Council to clarify the status of the priest *vis-à-vis* Church authority, on the one hand, and on the other what his position is vis-a-vis the people of God. There is no doubt that the Vatican Council has provided us with a developed understanding of the nature of Church, and of the place of each one of us – pope, bishops and people of God – within it. There has, however, always been a lingering doubt that the place of the priest was not clarified and needed to be looked at and developed. He is the middle man – the man who is the link between Christ and the people and at the same time, between Church authority and people.

Many of us have been so involved in the conveyor belt of the work and the continual distractions, demands and commitments we are involved in from day to day that we can barely spare time to stand back and to have a look at who we are and what our place is within the Church. We are probably the last of the GPs. Ray Brady tells us we have a sevenfold role – pastor, president, pray-er, teacher, counsellor, chairman/facilitator, administrator/manager.

It is for that reason that those of us who were members of the incoming Executive of NCPI in 1988 decided to take the theme of priest – his situation, his ministry, his person, his development – for a three-year period. A body like the NCPI can offer but very little. But we hoped that that little might be important and might make a small contribution in helping priests to pause and almost force a part-time commitment of all of us who are already over-stretched in our daily activities to look at our place within the Church.

LOOKING BACK: 1988 TO 1991

I want to look back very briefly at the last three years then and attempt to summarise what we have been trying to do.

From the outset, we acknowledged, like those who went before us, that if we are to communicate with our brother priests, those who are elected from each diocese, religious orders and missionary societies must communicate regularly with each other. Let me now state categorically that this has not happened in the past three years and it rarely happened in the twelve years before. This is a weakness. We have failed to put structures in place to enable this communication to take place. We believed we put them in place. We believed it could happen but it hasn't. In the early days when Bishop Larry Ryan was President of the NCPI, he and his Executive, through the *Handbook for Representatives*, suggested that representatives – diocesan, religious and missionary – in each diocese should meet at least twice a year and that one of them should be appointed a convener and that they should meet the bishop of the diocese at least once a year.

If something like this does not happen, it will be very difficult to get those we represent to reflect on some of the issues and topics which are touched on. Bishop Ryan, first President of NCPI said then:

The NCPI can be a force in the Irish Church. We have shown that we can speak clearly and calmly on behalf of the Irish clergy. The fact that we are elected by priests of every category from all age groups make us balanced and representative. It makes us into a forum where all shades of clerical opinion can be expressed. It places a discipline on us all to be open to views and experiences which differ from our own.

I regard that as an important statement and in this my last address to the NCPI, I want to link his words to the new delegates, to the new regional councils, to the new executive and to the new president.

Priests across Ireland realise that new initiatives are needed to meet the pastoral needs of the present and the years ahead. They also realise that their own role is changing. The theology of the priesthood has been changing. That change is partly the result of a new theological understanding of the Church and of ministries in the Church. It is influenced to a degree by new developments in the Church – in liturgy, catechesis, prayer, pastoral care of marriage and the family. It is partly too the outcome of the lived experiences of the priests and lay people in today's Church.

It is for this reason that the NCPI has been focussing on priest and priesthood since 1988. In this, it was conscious of being in harmony with the general movement, not just in Ireland, but throughout the Church worldwide.

The themes for the past three years have been: 'Being a Priest in Ireland Today (AGM 1988); 'Priest: Person and

Prophet' (AGM 1989); 'Priestly Development in a Changing World' (AGM 1990). The papers from the 1988 and 1990 Conferences have been published in book form.[1] Fr Damian Byrne's papers from the 1989 Conference are on video.[2]

A range of vital issues have been identified. The whole question of participative leadership has been one of these. An important function of the priest is to facilitate and promote leadership by others and to recognise precisely the exact kind of leadership which he himself must exercise. The question of priorities keeps coming up. For example, there have been a number of calls for a disentanglement of priests from aspects of educational administration which leave him less time for carrying out his pastoral ministry in schools. Over and over again, speakers and participants have been drawing attention to the need to recognise that priests are involved in activities which could be carried out by others and which leave the priest less time for carrying out his specifically priestly functions.

There is fairly widespread concern about priestly spirituality – in the context of prayer, but also in the area of priestly development.

The renewal of priests has always been a concern of this Conference and I think it can be said that many interesting

1. *Being a Priest in Ireland Today* (1989, Dublin, Dominican Publications, 96 pp., pbk); *Priestly Development in a Changing World* (1991, Dublin, Dominican Publications, 96 pp., pbk, £3.99).

2. The full text of both papers appears in *A Pilgrimage of Faith*, by Damian Byrne, O.P. (1991, Dublin, Dominican Publications, 143 pp., pbk, £5.99).

developments in this area over the last number of years have been inspired by the NCPI. Within Ireland, there has been an upsurge in interest in personal, parochial and diocesan renewal in many dioceses, within religious orders and missionary societies.

The Conference has continued to run its two ten-week renewal courses each year. In an effort to improve the process of renewal, the NCPI took a decision in April 1990 to set up a review committee with Bishop Laurence Ryan as chairman. A comprehensive report was prepared by this working party and Its conclusion.s have been offered to bishops, religious superiors, priest delegates of NCPI and others involved in formation in the hope that further reflection will take place, thus contributing to the work of renewal in the Church.

On behalf of the Executive and all the priests of Ireland, I wish to thank Bishop Ryan and the members of that committee on their work. They have produced a report which, in its analysis and recommendations, will prove to be, we believe a significant document for pastoral renewal in Ireland.[3]

The whole question of priorities – What should we be at? – kept coming up over the last few years. Working groups and regional meetings explored some of these priorities. For example, the northern region took the theme of preaching and in particular underlined some insights from Damian Byrne's talk at the AGM of 1990. The relevance of a statement like 'It is important to realise that through his dedication to preaching the priest himself becomes holy' was re-

3. The full text of the Ryan Report appears *infra*, pp. 113 to 122.

flected on in a prayerful atmosphere. The priests of the southern region decided to concentrate their energies on the school and the parish in the work of 'evangelisation'. This was felt to be a significant project and one which requires a lot of exploration. The eastern region at one stage organised a day for laity and priests around the theme of 'The Kingdom of God is best advanced by working together'.[4] Over two hundred people attended this seminar. The western region took a major initiative in carrying out a socio-economic study of twelve western communities. What was unique about the process of looking at local community was that priests and people came together to analyse, to design a framework for an initial social survey, to reflect and to indicate what they saw were the problems and potential in their own local community. It was a process embodying the community's ownership of its own analysis and proposals for its own future. This is one which commends itself on several different fronts and it is one I would like to spend a little bit of time on in the next part of my paper.

The NCPI has a number of working groups that worked on: The Life and Ministry of Priests; Pastoral Initiatives; Religious; Communications; Social Issues.

The Life and Ministry of Priests and Pastoral Initiatives Groups concentrated on the theme of the three years and formation which I have referred to above. The Working-group on Religious Priests looked at the representation of religious within NCPI and I think these elections have now been or-

4. Dr Werner Jeanrond's keynote paper from that Conference can be found in *Doctrine and Life*, July-August 1992

ganised on a much clearer and more definite basis. The Communications Group looked, for the most part, at how we communicate with our fellow-priests, with bishops and with the wider public. A highlight of the last few years has been the continuing good work of the Social Issues Group. It should be acknowledged that the NCPI is indebted to the overlap in the responsibilities of Fr Seán Healy from the CMRS Justice Desk. This group helped us to understand the social teaching of the Church and the links between the religious and social dimensions of life.

CHANGE

While there was a great need for concern with the priest and priestly development – and, I believe, great benefit has been derived from it – this must not deflect from our concern with the broader society and from our mission to comment on and to effect change within this society. If there is any one fact we have been reminded of more than any other in the past number of years, it is the fact of change. We are reminded that we are living in a completely different context from that of a generation ago. We have been experiencing many and varied attempts to build a world without God. How do we present the Good News in this kind of society? What kind of society is it that we live in? Back in 1988, as we started into this series of looking at priest and priesthood in Ireland, Bishop Donal Murray told us:

As we approach the twenty-first century, as we try to prepare the soil to receive the word, we, the Church in Ireland, need to be a community, fired by the mission of preaching the Gospel, of helping people to see the depth of the message and the joy of it and to see that it is worth almost complete commitment. To sustain that mission, we need a community which is evangelised and evangelising, catechised and catechising, reconciled and reconciling. Our role, whatever the details, will be to teach prayer, understanding and community.

There are phrases in that little paragraph which deserve some reflecting on phrases such as 'fired by the mission'; 'to see the depth of the message and the joy of it'; 'to see that it is worth almost complete commitment'.

Bishop Murray was right to remind us that to present the good news in its reasonableness and coherence in a way that makes sense to a world which is hungry for justice, love, peace, goodness, fortitude, responsibility and human dignity requires more than renewal courses. It requires an involvement in people's lives. Justice, peace, responsibility and love – these are all words which can come very cheap if they are spoken from outside.

Those of us who are visitors to Northern Ireland must in this context acknowledge that we do not understand the complexities of the situation here and we must pay tribute to those who do. They understand only because they have worked so closely with people on the ground and have shared in their pain.

The same has to be true for those who speak about poverty, unemployment or disillusionment, illness or bereavement. It has to be very true that those who are at one with people, those who are witnesses must have an enormous advantage in reflecting good news to the people.

Is there not enough evidence within society itself to suggest that centralised planning, power, control does not work? It has broken down in the USSR. It is not breaking down in high technology nations yet nor in the control big business has over governments and society. But there is enough evidence – unemployment, poverty, crime – to suggest it cannot last much longer here either. Vatican II gave us a clear understanding of the Church as one which must be participative. This concept of participation seems to be vital both within the Church and within society.

Maybe the key to looking at the future is best summed up in the statement of Alven Toffler in *Future Shock:*

> The time has come for a dramatic re-assessment of the direction of change, a re-assessment made not by the politicians or the sociologists or the clergy or the élitist revolutionaries, not by technicians or College Presidents, but by the people themselves. We need, quite literally, to 'go to the people' with a question that is almost never asked of them: What kind of society do you want 10, 20, 30 years from now?

We need to initiate, in short, a continuing plebiscite on the future. It has become clear in the USSR that centralised national planning simply does not work. We obviously have failed to realise that in many of the high technology nations, regardless of their political persuasion, the same centralised planning cannot work either. Surely the time is right for the formation in every society of a movement for total self-review, a public self-examination aimed at broadcasting and defining in social, as well as merely economic terms 'the goals of progress'. On the edge of a new millenium, on the brink of a new stage of human development, we are racing blindly into the future. But where do we want to go?

What would happen if we actually tried to answer this question? Imagine the power and evolutionary impact, if in every parish in Ireland we set aside the next five years as a period of intense national self-appraisal from the ground up; if at the end of five years we were to come forward with our own agenda for the future, a programme embracing not merely economic targets but equally important broad sets of social goals with values and principles which emerge from the Gospel of Jesus Christ in guiding us. What would happen if such a grass-roots movement enabling large numbers of hitherto unconsulted people to express themselves and in effect become the policy makers of the future in which the people help shape their own distant destinies?

Michael D. Higgins is right when he suggests that people in Europe would be horrified if they thought that democracy is only an illusion. The world rejoices with developments towards democracy in Russia. But what does democracy mean in Ireland? What say have people in determining the present or future? To some, this appeal for a form of plebiscite will no doubt seem naive. Yet nothing Is more naive than the notion that we can continue to run the society the way we do at present. To some, it will appear impractical. Yet nothing is more impractical than the attempt to impose a humane future from above. What was naive under industrialism may be realistic in the post industrial era; what was practical may be absurd.

Could I even suggest further that the priest in Ireland could still be well enough positioned at local level to set this in motion. Certainly, no other organisation has an officer in each local area Why is this concept beginning to make more sense?

To understand what is happening to us and what kind of society we have is not easy. On the one hand, we point to the extraordinary achievements in art, science, intellectual, moral and political life, and at the same time point to the fact that tens of thousands of young people live reality by opting for drug inducements of one kind or another, a society in which big numbers of parents retreat into video-induced stupor or alcoholic haze, a society in which big numbers of elderly people vegetate and die in loneliness, a society in which the family as we knew it is coming under severe pressure. Many of us have a vague feeling that things are moving very fast. Doctors and executives alike complain that they cannot keep up with the latest developments in their fields. Hardly a meeting or conference takes place today without some ritualistic oratory about 'the challenge of change'. Among many, there is an uneasy mood – a suspicion that change is out of control.

Big numbers do not share this anxiety at all. They live their lives as if nothing had changed and as if nothing ever will. They will say that youth was always rebellious and that what is happening today is no different from the past. So many of us, of course, have been so ignorant about the past that we see nothing unusual about the present. A disturbing fact is that the vast majority of us find the idea of change so threatening that we attempt to deny its existence. Even many people who understand intellectually that change is accelerating, do not take this critical fact into account in planning their own personal lives.

In short, the evidence is all around us. Centralised power simply does not work any more. People must be given responsibility if they are to grow and develop. Strong government, big organisations, large industry and business – control by the few all lead to cynicism and eventual breakdown.

CHALLENGE TO CHRISTIANITY

We now stand at the threshold of the third millenium of the Christian era and between two very critical decades. In 1992 we become very much part of an integrated European unit with the introduction of the single market. This will have economic, but also moral and political implications. It may help to refer to two issues: unemployment and the world of business.

On the social side, clearly Ireland's major problem today is unemployment. With over 350,000 (north and south) out of work and with the proposed single European market posing serious questions for peripheral countries, there is a clear obligation for everyone to contribute to a solution and to be allowed to do so.

As the absolute numbers and rate of unemployment rise to 20% of the work force and to 80% in some urban estates, we must recognise a paralysis both in thought and action in dealing with the problem. In the south, young talented people must follow our £2 billion annual debt repayment out of the country. At least 100,000 people are now unemployed for one year or more of which 25,000 are unemployed more than three years. Ten years ago, our concern was with youth unemployment. We did not solve it, but its victims got older and shifted the problem into the 25 to 44 age-group. In another ten or fifteen years, there will be a sector of a generation of Irish people coming to the end of their working lives who will never have had a job.

What is more noteworthy than our failure in this area is our refusal to acknowledge the failure. There is no evidence of innovation or creative approaches to the problem emanating from the large public bodies charged with development and job creation.

Such development agencies are inadequately scrutinised in terms of their effectiveness and their contribution to the Irish society. Instead of such scrutiny, the public receives a continuous diet of bland PR exercises, which are little more than a cynical attempt to obscure the failures of such agencies to deliver on what they are set up to do.

The society we are now part of is heavily influenced by

'big business'. Moralists have tended to write on professional ethics but little on business ethics. This is strange since business tends to impinge so greatly on all our lives. Business conduct appears to be governed by a code of ethics, but only in so far as that code is enshrined in the law of the land or the standards adopted by the community in which the business person operates. The approach adopted suggests that if business practice is not illegal, it is thereby ethically acceptable.

It is true that when a business does not produce real economic wealth, the competitive environment in which we live punishes it severely. However, we have been experiencing the emergence of some strange developments in the business world, such as shell companies, paper money, etc. – operations which have made no real contribution to the creation of economic wealth or employment.

It must now be clear that the problems of achieving justice and charity in Irish society cannot be solved by fiscal measures alone. The time is opportune to explore what the Gospel has to say to this world and to encourage Christian business people to produce a formal code of ethics so that their personal code of behaviour may be checked against an objective written code.

THE NEED FOR DEBATE

One has to be disturbed at the depth and extent of cynicism in Ireland in relation to civic issues. Public spirit is either lacking or, where it is present, it is distrusted or disbelieved.

Without a broadly based, generalised civic morality, Irish society will degenerate into anarchy. Leadership, not only at the political level but also in the business, education and religious worlds must set the standards of civic morality. Their claim to public leadership is otherwise invalid.

Irish people need to be discussing those and other issues in a comprehensive way and in a way which they feel impacts on decisions and on the direction of public life. As things stand, there is no forum for such a debate. The public service media which began a great tradition of debate in the 1960s have allowed such debate to degenerate in many cases to little more than tabloid titillation. There is no innovative analysis coming forward. Established organisations and interests come forward with established clichés.

The forum is urgently required where people can regain their sense of democracy; which can allow the fundamental decency of Irish people to assert itself and which can appraise where we are as a society and where we are heading. We need structures which can engage meaningful and comprehensive participation by people in discussing their problems and in identifying possible solutions. We need to transform the hopeless and destructive cynicism of the population into a force which has vitality and is purposeful, humane and tolerant.

ACTIVE FOR MISSION

In the Ireland of the pre-1960s when our society was stable and stagnant, out of the main stream of modern life and modern politics, the Church was the only institution offering an ideal to young people. It looked out to the wider world and called on young people to do something about the paganism and poverty in which most of humanity lived. It received a wonderful response – between the middle of the nineteenth and the twentieth century the number of priests increased six-fold, and the number of nuns rose even faster. By 1950, the number of priests on the missions equalled the number of priests on the home front. This was an expanding, confident Church. Its pastoral, spiritual, administrative and managerial achievements, at home and abroad, in education, health, welfare, deserve the highest recognition.

We are now part of a society which looks out at the world and we must ask how we as a Church are called on to become active again for mission and not confine ourselves to introspective analysis and the carrying out merely of a maintenance operation.

Our hope is that this conference will help us discover not only what the message of salvation is but how people are helped to live out the salvation which Christ has bestowed on them.

The Pastoral Challenge of Social Change

Liam Ryan

> But it seems that something has
> happened that has never happened before:
> though we know not just when, or why,
> or how, or where.
> Men have left God not for other gods,
> they say, but for no god; and this has
> never happened before.
> T.S. Eliot, 'Choruses from *The Rock*'

> There is nothing more the Vatican, the bishops or we
> priests can do to drive the laity out of the Church. We did
> everything we could – and often continue to do it – and
> still they won't go.
> Andrew Greeley, *America*, August 1987

About four years ago RTÉ presented four *Radharc* programmes on Dutch Catholicism. The first focussed on the decline of religion in Holland as the inevitable consequence of the secularization trends of modern western society, and predicted that what was happening today in Holland may well occur in Ireland or Southern Italy by the end of the century. The second programme, in contrast, saw the decline as due to human error, mistaken appointments by Rome, attempts to hold the Church together by power and authority, and a reversion to an outmoded traditionalism.

Which explanation was accurate? Possibly both, since history is fashioned by people themselves as well as by social, economic or cultural forces. However, let us first look at the forces that have brought such profound social changes to modern society.

INDUSTRIALIZATION

No medieval man or woman awoke one morning and suddenly declared themselves modern. What we call modernity is a process that has sprung from many sources, and while it is conventional to date it to the French Revolution, that event was more a sign of its presence than a proclamation of its birth. More accurately it could be said to have begun in 1769 when James Watt harnessed the expansive power of steam for human use. Economic production took a giant step forward, and during the next two centuries industrialization acted as the chief catalyst in hastening the transformation of society.

The greatest defeat of modern Christianity was its failure in the industrial revolution. Pope Pius XI was right to call this the 'great scandal' of the nineteenth century, for the failure not only brought about the ruin of the Church in Europe which had been its home, it also provided a precedent for the decline of religion in industrialized societies everywhere. What was involved was more than shortages in the provision of churches and clergy in the new industrial towns and suburbs. It was also a failure of theology. Society had become mobile but the social philosophy and theology implied by the official religion had not. In the mid-nineteenth century, the Anglican divine, social reformer and novelist, Charles Kingsley, told his English readers: 'We have used the Bible as if it were a special constable's handbook, an opium dose for keeping beasts of burden patient while they were being overloaded, a mere book to keep the poor in order.' Christianity's institutional failure was likely to vary with the size of the city: an aspect of the industrial city that has persisted into the twentieth century.

Ireland largely escaped the worst features of the industrial age in that the mass migration of impoverished rural dwellers from the Irish countryside, both in this century and in the last, was not to Irish cities but to Britain and America where they helped to swell the ranks of the urban poor. Indeed in his description of conditions in Manchester in 1844, Frederic Engels drew a horrifying portrait of 'Little Ireland', a slum which was a disgrace even for the Manchester of those days. By and large, rural migrants to Irish cities seldom enter the urban arena at the bottom. Indeed, Dublin is unique in Europe in that a higher percentage of its citizens were born in the capital than is true of any other capital city in Europe.

There are three comments I wish to make on the impact of industrialization on Ireland. The first is that many of the worst features of nineteenth century urban poverty are now being recreated in Irish cities. In Dublin, in particular, the disappearance of thousands of unskilled and semi-skilled jobs over the past three decades has left a large section, especially of the male population, practically unemployable. The policy of dispersal of industrial jobs to every locality in Ireland, meant that since 1970 Dublin has lost some 15,000 industrial jobs while the rest of the country has gained. The result is the emergence of communities in Dublin, both in the suburbs and the inner-city where unemployment has become a way of life for most of the residents. More significantly, this new poverty and unemployment is taking on many of the features of Victorian poverty, including a substantial drift away from religion. The poorer areas of Irish cities today offer one of the great challenges to the Catholic Church in Ireland, a challenge that few countries in Europe have successfully met. The Irish Church's great achievement in the past, unlike much of Europe, was to retain the loyalty of the working class. Today it is rapidly losing it.

My second observation is that Ireland coped with the problems of transition from a traditional to a modern society largely through the safety mechanism of emigration. Emigration is at the centre of the Irish experience of being modern. The transition has been made possible by the simple expedient of Ireland offering a modern way of life to 75% of its population. The remaining 25% have had, for a long time past, a choice of unemployment at home or migration abroad. They have always generously chosen to promote the welfare of the 75% at home by opting to leave rather than stay. Consequently, emigration is a mirror in which the Irish nation can see its true face, especially as in Ireland alone does emigration persist with a nineteenth century intensity.

My third point is that while emigration was not unique to Ireland, in no other country was emigration so essential a prerequisite for the preservation of the nature of the society. The three forces that by and large created modern Ireland – political nationalism, the Catholic Church, and the middle class, both urban and rural – have always been traditionalist and conservative. As Kevin O'Higgins said of national independence in 1926, 'We were the most conservative revolutionaries in history'. All three forces combined to attempt something never thought possible anywhere else in the world: to become a modern and perhaps an industrial society while retaining the basic structure of society intact. We may have become modern but our conservative politics, our traditionalist religion and our reactionary middle classes have maintained their position and their power largely because many of the forces for change left Ireland with the 25% of the population condemned to emigration. Emigration has for two centuries been the safety valve of Irish society removing overseas the dispossessed and the disinherited, the unemployed and the overpopulated, the marginal and the radical, the alienated and the frustrated, whose departure took away a major force for social change and made possible the continuation of a cohesive, traditional society.

The prospect today, and one that offers a major challenge to the Church, is that we have a rapidly growing section of the population, largely young, who will not be integrated by the twin ideologies of Catholicism and nationalism nor by the promise of a good life in terms of jobs, marriage, houses and the benefits of a consumer society. With the twin mechanisms of emigration and borrowing no longer operable, this section of the population is likely to become a major problem for themselves and for the entire Irish nation.

PLURALISM

Before religion is thought of as a creed, it is offered as a prayer; and before it is offered as a prayer it is experienced as a community. Put more simply, we obtain our notions about the world originally from other human beings, and these notions continue to be plausible to us in very large measure because others to affirm them. It is, of course, possible to go against the social consensus that surrounds us, but there are powerful pressures to conform to the views and beliefs of our fellow men and women. In short, what people actually find credible largely depends on the social support they receive.

Thus relating to any belief or opinion we hold, whether political, religious or cultural, we can speak of plausibility structures, meaning the strength of the supporting evidence. Thus, for example, the maintenance of the Catholic faith in the consciousness of an individual requires a community of Catholics in one's social milieu who constantly support this faith. Societies vary in their capacity to provide such firm plausibility structures for religious belief. Clearly, the capacity steadily diminishes as one moves from ancient to

modern society and from a closed rural community to an urban industrial world. Most individuals in traditional society
lived in tribes or clans or communities where the interpretation of reality, including religion was taken to be natural, inevitable and self-evident. The modern individual exists in a
plurality of worlds, migrating back and forth between competing and often contradictory plausibility structures, each
of which is weakened by the simple fact of its involuntary
coexistence with other plausibility structures.

Pluralism is a term that originated in the United States,
and refers to the empirically obvious situation that American society has been a product of a great plurality of ethnic,
racial and religious groups. But in origin much of modern
religious pluralism derives from the Protestant Reformation
and its subsidiary schisms and sub-divisions. What pluralism brings is that people begin to have a choice as to their
religious affiliation and this can happen even in countries
with a high degree of homogeneity such as Sweden, for example. Generally speaking, the modern world has provided
a multiplication of options in human life. Modernization, in
terms of the basic religious affiliations that one holds, has
meant a movement from fate to choice.

When religion ceases to be a matter of fate and becomes
a matter of choice, there are some fundamental changes in
the manner in which religion is maintained in the consciousness of individuals. Put simply, religion becomes a less certain matter. When the gods become a matter of choice, they
become a much less objective reality, they become more of

a subjective matter, they become a matter of taste, of opinion, of change.

Through much of our recent history Ireland both politically and religiously was marked by a convergence or consensus whose plausibility structures were firmly in place. Emmet Larkin, a historian of the University of Chicago, traces this process in terms of an alignment between Church, State and Nation in seven stages since the middle of the last century with the various elements developing, growing and converging until they finally merge in the late nineteen thirties:

1. The pragmatic loyalty of the Church to constituted authority: initially the Church and the British State working together.
2. The growing self-confidence of the Catholic middle classes – the growth of the Nation.
3. The increased identification of the clergy with the Catholic middle classes – the alignment of Church and Nation.
4. The merging of Catholic and National identities: Larkin's so-called 'devotional revolution' when the Irish became militantly Catholic.
5. The politicisation of Irish identity – the middle classes seeking their rights: the Land League and Home Rule.
6. The New Nationalism and the New State.
7. The Constitution of 1937 – a symbol of the final merger of Church, State and Nation.

The degree to which that alignment or consensus is now

gone is a matter of opinion. Certainly to many observers, Ireland now exhibits many of the characteristics of a pluralist state, perhaps even a secular state, dominated more by economic than religious or national considerations. Many of the old certainties have gone – the belief in the Catholic Church as the one true Church of Christ, rock-firm, unchanging, to which people were expected to look for certainties, for detailed rules of behaviour, for the answers to all life's problems.

It is a sobering thought that the great changes of the early 1960s, Vatican II, on the one hand, and Seán Lemass on the other, are outside the personal experience of anyone in this country under 35 years or so. And that is more than half the people of Ireland. These people do not know what life was like in Catholic Ireland before the Council. They have not experienced the narrowness of attitude; the censorship; the infallibility not of popes but of bishops, parish priests and curates; the obsession with the evils of dancing; the multiplication of mortal sins, as if there were not sufficient already; above all the presentation of life as a sort of process in which living did not matter but only the passing of the final examination.

Pluralism, especially as portrayed in the immense growth in the volume and immediacy of communications, has two consequences that are of immediate importance to religion.

The first is that religion is now a matter of competition not inheritance. The pastoral implications here are enormous for Irish Catholicism. In the past the pastoral techniques of the Church largely depended on having influence through having control. In today's world the Church must learn how to have influence without control, and that means being open, being honest, being accountable – not exactly characteristics one immediately associates with the clerical Church.

One can judge how well the Irish Church performs in a modern pluralist world by asking how seriously it takes the fact that it is in a highly competitive situation. The Irish Church is probably unique in that it still retains the goodwill of the people of Ireland. Those who no longer practice have not so much lost faith as hope that the Church has anything to say or to offer to them. Women call for change in a Church which treats them as second-class citizens. But youth and the laity generally could make the same complaint. Male geriatric dictatorship may well have been what finally toppled Communism in Eastern Europe. There must be a lesson there somewhere for a Church that seeks not merely to survive but to transform humanity.

The second point of importance in a pluralist world is that today's people are influenced more by the wisdom of one's words than by the dignity of one's office. Dogmatism is questioned, as better education and foreign travel create a greater openness to new ideas and values. Clerical paternalism and authoritarianism are resented as people are no longer satisfied with the old formulations and formulae. A Christianity that is seen as a code and not a community will certainly not appeal. A Church which is constantly condemning rather than uplifting will not influence many. This is a problem particularly in Ireland where the Church has a real dilemma in areas of social morality. While it must take a stand in line with Catholic teaching on issues of contraception and divorce, as Bishop Donal Murray says:

> If bishops and Church spokes-persons are perceived as constantly opposing these demands, the result may be to confirm the image of religion as obscurantist and of the Church as an institution protecting its own power. This could strengthen, rather than promote critical reflection on, these demands. The values of tolerance, freedom and compassion which underpin the liberal stance are real values which the Church must not be seen to ignore. Many people, including many good Catholics, may be unnecessarily alienated if these new currents, liberalism, feminism, pluralism and so on are approached in terms of mere condemnation rather than as cultural realities to be deepened, enlightened and, where necessary, purified in the light of the Gospel. Any criticism which is perceived to be lacking in tolerance, compassion and love of freedom will be counterproductive.

Put simply, if the Catholic faith is to survive with strength and vitality in Ireland we must be seen more in terms of what we are for rather than of what we are against.

SECULARISATION

There have been many descriptions of the age in which we live – modern, industrial, urban, secular, liberal, pluralist, godless, technological. Running through many of the descriptions is the idea of a world that can do without the Godhead because it has discovered its own manhood. Pope Leo XIII when he condemned 'Americanism' in 1899 linked that heretical tendency with the suggestion that 'the Church should adapt herself more to the civilization of a world that has reached the age of manhood.' The idea of the world's 'coming of age' has a long history, for the comparison of the life of mankind with the life of an individual has been around a long time in literature and rhetoric. As a catchphrase to describe the process of secularization, recent discussion of the phrase 'coming of age' has centered around its use by the German Protestant theologian Dietrich Bonhoeffer in a letter from prison in June 1944.

Basically it refers to modern man's sense that his powers are increasing and that, however inadequate they may be at present, his only real hope lies in their increase, for no greater power will help him. As man's consciousness of his powers, or at least of his potential, has grown, so his reliance on supernatural force has shrunk, or at least has been seen to need a radical readjustment and restatement. Traditionally *homo sapiens* was *homo religiosus* for he needed divine help to survive, to hunt animals and to rear his children. In the twentieth century increasing numbers of people have either experienced no such need of supernatural force, or else they have believed that it would be futile to expect their need to be satisfied as a consequence of prayer.

That there has been a shift of emphasis in modern civilization can scarcely be doubted. When modern people feel sick, they want medicine; when their crops are poor, they want fertilisers; when they are ignorant, they want education; and when they want rain, they do not beat drums. Despite all its problems, optimism has continued to be the prevailing note of the western world in the twentieth century. And it has been basically an optimism in what humanity can accomplish for itself.

The point in presenting this aspect of modernity is that central to it is the view that from primitive magic to the prayer of the Christian to a heavenly Father for daily bread, the central theme of religion could be expressed as a cry for help. As a consequence, it is argued that it is crucial for the future of religion that its defenders should see that the main weight of their case can no longer rest on the weakness of man; instead, most of the case for religion. must now be built on the recognition of man's great strength.

There are two ways of looking at the whole process of secularization, that process by which sectors of society and culture are removed from the influence of religious interpretation. The first is to see it as desacralization, as a breaking away from religion and its influence and turning one's attention from other worlds to this one. A second and more positive approach to the subject is to see secularization as the result of a transformation of the self-understanding of what it means to be human. Mankind perceives itself as a creative subject, as an agent of history responsible for its own destiny. From a cosmological vision, humanity moves to an anthropological vision which brings in its wake a different way of conceiving one's relationship with God. In this sense, secularization can be in harmony with a Christian vision of mankind, of history, of the universe. The Bible affirms that creation is distinct from the Creator; it is the proper sphere of humanity, whom God himself has proclaimed lord of this creation. To work with this creation offers mankind the possibility of being fully human.

What does all this mean in practice? Simply that rather than define the world in terms of the religious phenomenon, we should rather define religion in relation to the secular. If formerly the tendency was to see the world in terms of the Church, today almost the reverse is true, the Church is seen in terms of the world.

What is called for is a new humility and a new flexibility on the part of the Church. This would mean a recognition that theology is not something finished and given, not even something in constant need of remaking through the personal confrontation of knowing Christians with the truth of Christ and his Church, but more importantly in confrontation with the secular world also. This would involve a recognition of the secular world as a worthy part of God's and man's creation, a world entitled to exist and be interpreted in its own right. In short, a recognition that there are legitimate boundaries between the sacred and the secular as narrowly interpreted. Pastorally, it would mean starting from where people are, indeed starting from where the Church is with all its doubts and fears and inadequacies.

'OPEN CATHOLICISM'

How, then, has the Irish Church coped with the process of modernity and social change? The answer is that it has coped remarkably well at the organisational level, not so well at fashioning the type of individual Catholic capable of coping with modern society. It is perhaps an over-simplification to state that the specifically lay contribution to a distinctively Irish Catholicism has been the one the rest of the Catholic world now accepts as a model, the specifically clerical contribution is one that even Ireland itself is now rejecting.

Despite Irish Catholics' tradition of deference to their pastors, the clergy have never been able to count on the obedience of their flock on all issues. This is particularly true in the political arena where the slogan 'We will take our religion from Rome but our politics from Home' has long summed up the native attitude on issues where there occurred a clash between what the clergy considered permissible and what public opinion was prepared to tolerate.

This trait in Irish Catholicism – the ability to profess loyalty to the Church while rejecting its guidance on particular issues – is at least as old as the Fenian movement in the 1860s. One historian, John A. Murphy of University College, Cork, has suggested that it was due to an individualistic tradition in Irish piety:

The private and devotional nature of Irish Catholicism provided a solution to the dilemma of the Catholic revolutionary: he could argue that while the priest's spiritual authority must be respected, politics was none of his business. (*Christus Rex*, October, 1959, p. 254)

This ability to remain loyal to the Church in some matters and not in others marks out Ireland from other Catholic countries. Elsewhere, a rejection of clerical views on one issue has led to a questioning of clerical views in general. As the historian, John H. Whyte states:

Ireland is exceptional among Catholic countries in that it has never produced an anti-clerical party. The reason is not that Irish Catholics are uniformly docile, but that they are able to compartmentalise their loyalties, and to accept the Church's authority unquestioningly in one sphere at the very time that they challenge it in another. (*Church and State in Modern Ireland*, p. 12)

This tradition of independence of clerical guidance on political matters is at the basis of Ireland's greatest contribution to modern Catholicism. In the nineteenth century, Ireland, being the only Catholic English speaking nation, had to come to terms with the problem of how to live in an essentially Protestant and increasingly secular world. It evolved a Catholic liberalism of 'a free Church in a free State', an idea it exported to the English-speaking world and which eventually became an integral part of Vatican II theology. This tradition was very much out of line with papal teaching in the nineteenth century, the principle of the separation of Church and State being condemned by Gregory XVI in 1832, by Pius IX in his Syllabus of Errors of 1864, and later by Leo XIII in two encyclicals.

We can appreciate the Irish contribution all the more if we contrast the 'closed Catholicism' of continental Europe with the 'open Catholicism' of the Anglo-American world. In the former, Catholic life prior to Vatican II was organised on an exclusively confessional basis; Catholics joined exclusively Catholic organisations and had a political party which received the support of all Catholics; indeed, the clergy repeatedly told their people that it was their moral duty to vote for the Catholic party. In the Anglo-American tradition of open-Catholicism no such arrangement exists; Catholics divide their support among multiple parties; the clergy stay aloof from politics, and few exclusively Catholic organisations such as trade unions exist. As the circumstances which fostered the growth of closed Catholicism die away, continental Catholicism has also turned to a model of Church-State relations and of religion-society relations pioneered by Irish Catholicism in the nineteenth century.

It is interesting to note that this tradition of open Catholicism in Ireland extended beyond the the political arena to some areas but not to others. For instance, there was never an attempt in Ireland to establish a comprehensive Catholic press nor exclusively Catholic trade unions. On the other hand, in areas such as education or mixed marriages Ireland tended to follow the continental closed-Catholicism model.

PATERNALISM

It is odd that a Church which created a model of organisa-

tion based on the confidence to allow its members a free rein
in matters of politics and social organisation should have ex-
hibited such paternalism to its flock in other areas of human
living. This is especially true of two spheres which the
Church traditionally regards as its peculiar preserve – education and the family. The four deadly sins of Irish Catholicism all relate to these areas of life: an obsession with sexual
morality, clerical authoritarianism, anti-intellectualism or at
best non-intellectualism, and the creation of a ghetto mentality. While these are to some extent clichéd criticisms,
there is perhaps a number of reasons which led both Church
and State in Ireland, in the decades after independence, to
collaborate in dragooning citizens into virtuous living.

There was a strain of lofty puritanism in the new nationalism which inspired the founding fathers. A self-governing
Ireland would not be a prosperous Ireland but something of
a republic of virtue as well, an island of saints if not of
scholars. In addition, a key concept in Irish Catholic nationalism had long been the rejection of 'alien' literature and
philosophies from a post-Christian Europe and a pagan
neighbour. What more logical, then, than to use the legisla-
tive powers of a homogeneously Catholic State to exclude
the 'alien' influences and strengthen the indigenous virtue?

Furthermore, it is important in that era to note the role of
paternalism in both Church and State. The Church, in particular, tended to see its flock as the 'simple faithful', existing in a permanent state of childhood, to be preserved in a
moral quarantine against alien contamination and domestic

occasions of sin. Whatever differences may have existed between Church and State, both parties were agreed, so to speak, not to fight in front of the children. One of the last great expressions of clerical paternalism was Archbishop John Charles McQuaid's statement to his flock on returning from the first session of the Vatican Council. He said: 'You may have been worried by much talk of changes to come. Allow me to reassure you. No change will worry the tranquility of your Christian lives.'

Social Policies and Social Attitudes in Northern Ireland

Maurice Hayes

The theme of the conference is ministry in a divided society. I propose to talk mainly about Northern Ireland and to deal mainly with those aspects of division which arise from poverty, disadvantage and deprivation rather than the more commonly observed divisions resulting from sectarian and political conflicts. These latter have already been reasonably covered and there will be others better placed to comment on them than I. It is one of the minor tragedies of the present situation that concentration on the sectarian and political conflicts has tended to occlude discussion on the very real divisions in this society and the very real problems of the 'have nots' in a society which is divided by wealth and class and opportunity.

It is an irony of contemporary politics that in Ireland, a country characterised by the youngest population in the European community – and that population in any case half female – social policy tends to be made by groups and interests in which middle-aged or elderly males predominate. Not only that but the lessons they learn tend to have been based on the experience of at least a generation earlier. They tend to be better at countering the problems of the last generation (which may indeed no longer be problems) than anticipating those of the next. They do generally have very real problems in communicating with the younger generation; they are usually better equipped for transmission of messages than for the reception of views, information or concern, and not only changes in social attitudes and perceptions but changes in the use of language make any sort of meaningful dialogue across age, class and social divisions extremely difficult. And being not only middle-aged but middle-class and middle-minded it is no surprise that any coincidence between social policies and the reality of the social problems faced by ordinary people in the real world is at best a haphazard affair.

I do not wish to draw an immediate analogy between the field of social policy and the pastorate, but pastors should be aware of the social and economic context in which they work, and should use demography and social research as an essential tool. You need to know what is happening in social and economic terms to the communities and individuals you work with, and, in a time of rapid social change, you need to be aware of trends. There is a danger too that institutional policies may be based on perception of what the position or problem was a generation ago and may not accord to the reality on the ground today.

I am not sure to what extent people rely on parish surveys or censuses and to what extent these are more than a mere head count. All I want to encourage you to do is to look at the larger picture – at what appears to sociologists and policy makers to be happening in society generally in Northern Ireland (and in Ireland) and to provide some sort of context into which you might place your own consideration of your work. The census has been taken this year North and South. The first crude figures are just now available, not yet fully analysed. Reports will be coming out periodically over the next two years giving further analysis and breaking the figures down by district and otherwise.

There is also valuable information in social surveys such as *Social Trends* (in the United Kingdom.) *Social Brief* (in Northern Ireland and including data from the Continuous Household Survey), *Social Attitudes in Northern Ireland* (recently published by Blackstaff), opinion polls and other surveys.

We live in changing times, and apart from adapting pastoral approaches to the challenges, the problems and the possibilities connected with the change, clergy of all denominations need to have some idea of the appropriateness of the method used, of the deployment of manpower (and womanpower) and of the changing needs, desires and attitudes of people.

TRENDS

The main trends I would ask you to consider:are:

Demographic: Changes in the make-up of the population: age structure, birth rates, life expectancy, proportion of the population in each age/generation band, dependency rates, migration and demigration.

Locational: Where people live, urban or rural, in community or isolated, emigration.

Economic: Changes in how and where people work, in employment/unemployment trends, in fair employment, in how work in allocated in society, in what determines development, in central planning or market forces.

Attitudinal: Changes to a variety of social and moral issues including family, religion, sexual morality.

Changes in society and social policy: Pluralisation, de-institutionalisation, individualism, mobility, the decline of the extended family.

POPULATION CHANGES

In Northern Ireland present population trends could be used to predict that over the next ten years there will be a decrease in births by 3.5%. However, if trends in the Republic of Ireland and the United Kingdom and the rest of the EC are followed, the collapse in fertility rates could come much more quickly. What has been most marked over the last decade has been the rapid fall in fertility rates among Catholic women (even more marked in the South than in the North) and in Northern Ireland a trend towards the convergence of Catholic and Protestant fertility rates. And although Catholic families on average are larger the difference is reducing. Currently the average Roman Catholic family size is 3.4, the average Protestant family 2.7. 29% of Roman Catholic families are likely to number more than five compared with 12% of Protestants.

Other trends are of an increase of 4.5% over the period in children of primary school age and an increase of 5.5% in the 10-14 age band and 5.25% in the band 15-64 years. These figures will impact on the need for school places and the numbers of young people coming into the labour market.

There will be a decrease of 2.5% of the number of people in the 65-74 age band but much more significantly an increase of 11% in the number of people surviving to 75 years and over. This perhaps is the most significant figure. All over the developed world populations are growing older. Ireland, north and south, has the highest proportion of young people in northern European countries where fertility rates are not in most cases securing replacement and where populations are ageing rapidly. More and more young people are surviving into their 80s and 90s and in many countries attitudes to retirement and to the elderly are having to be rethought and the elderly, especially where concentrated as in Florida and the south cost of England, are becoming important political lobbies. The offence of ageism is now being added to those of racism and sexism.

For pastoral workers in Ireland I suggest the most immediate visible impact may be in community care. Increasingly, in a society which still depends on family members (and inordinately on female family members) for social care of the elderly, there is the prospect of the elderly 80- or 90-year-old being looked after by daughters who are themselves in their 60s and 70s. Who cares for carers in these circumstances? And increasing age brings with it increasing incidence of the conditions associated with age – immobility and dementia.

TOWN AND COUNTRY

The single most marked population trend in Ireland north and south in the present century has been urbanisation, the movement of people from country to towns and inordinately to Dublin and the Belfast area.

In the Republic one in three people lived in towns of 10,000 population at work in 1901. By 1986 this was almost exactly reversed, only one in three people living outside towns. However, this pattern has not been evenly spread – 67.2% of town dwellers live in Leinster, only 5% in Connaught.

The most notable feature is the absolute dominance of Dublin. The population of the Dublin metropolitan area exceeds the aggregate of the next nineteen large towns. Cork, the next largest, although growing, is only one-fifth the size of Dublin.

The same pattern is found in Northern Ireland but less dramatically. 43% of the population lived in towns in 1901, 64% today. Again the dominance of Belfast is marked with one-third of the population of Northern Ireland in the Greater Belfast area and Belfast more than six times as big as the next town.

And coming up fast are the changes to the rural economy, north and south, which will result from changes in the Common Agricultural Policy, the diminishing economic importance of farming, the loss of wealth and employment in rural areas and the possible de-stabilisation of traditional rural communities.

What is of greater significance is what is happening within Belfast and Dublin. In both cases the core is shrinking, there is population loss in the inner city and growth in the suburbs and peripheral estates.

In Dublin the population of the inner city (within the canals) which was 85% of the borough population (and 56% of the metropolitan population) in 1926 is now 16.6% and 8.2%. In other words where more than four out of five city-people lived in 1926, now fewer than one in six lives or only one in twelve of the metropolitan population.

In Belfast the change has been more dramatic in recent years. Between 1971 and 1985 the Greater Belfast area population as a whole declined by 30%. However, the built-up area around the city increased by 22%; the City Council area declined by 22%; the inner city declined by 49%; Protestant households in the centre of the city declined by 15%; Catholic households by 10%.

The effect has been an inner city population characterised by high proportion of elderly; high unemployment; high dependency on social welfare; poor environment; poor health; poverty and relative deprivation.

In Belfast and Dublin too there is the legacy of large public housing estates in the '60s and '70s and mainly the result of city centre clearance and redevelopment, the decanting of inner city populations to green-field sites on the periphery.

These tended to lack social and other amenities. Basic urban infrastructures like schools and churches and shops were late in coming, and public transport to link with the city centre was either inadequate or nonexistent. In an age of planning dominated by catering for the two-car family the non-car owner was isolated and deprived and if he lived in the inner city was being asked to pay the social and environmental costs of providing free-way access to the city centre for the commuter and shoppers. The result is a mosaic of new housing areas which replicate many of the disadvantages of the inner city. Populations are younger, it is true, with overcrowding and high dependency ratios. But there is also high dependency on social welfare, high levels of unemployment, low levels of education and attainment, low levels of skill, poor health, poor environment, poverty and relative deprivation.

UNEMPLOYMENT

Unemployment rates in Northern Ireland are not likely to improve significantly over the next few years. In one sense we are running fast to stand still. Government job creation agencies not surprisingly prefer to talk in terms of job creation and ask us to look at the number of people in employment which has been increasing rather than the numbers in the unemployment register which have also been rising. The equation is complex. For part of the explanation is the increased number of young people coming on to the labour market and fluctuations in the rate of emigration as opportunities close down through recession in the UK and US labour markets. There is also the problem that one job created does not equate to an equal reduction in the unemployment register. Indeed Graham Gudgeon has argued that it takes three new jobs to remove one person from the unemployed register. The others will be filled by a woman becoming economically active or by new entrants to the labour market.

Up to the end of 1990 the Northern Ireland economy had been expanding at the rate of 8,000 jobs a year (36,000 in four years) which just kept unemployment at the same level during the period. However, in the same period 26,000 people more left Northern Ireland than came in reducing unemployment from 17.7% to 13.7% (although it has since risen to 14%). This is not likely to be sustained. Slow growth in the United Kingdom economy will be reflected in Northern Ireland, and in Britain and the United States there will be fewer opportunities for Northern Ireland people. Jobs are now expected to be created at a rate of 3,000 a year throughout the 1990s. Out-migration will reduce from 8,000 to 4,000 a year. Unemployment on this prediction would rise to 15% in 1991-92 and remain at that level.

As in the past, general unemployment statistics will continue to conceal local pockets of endemic unemployment at very much higher rates and these pockets are likely to be found in the inner city and the peripheral urban estates.

As a result of fair employment legislation and other action, institutional discrimination has been outlawed and considerable progress made in opening up the labour market. However, the results of historic discriminatory practices remain and the more intractable structural problems of location, education, skills mix and labour markets and practices are still likely to produce significant differences between the communities in employment patterns.

Of those in work, 31% are Catholic, although Catholics are significantly less likely than Protestants to hold managerial positions and are over-represented in the semi-skilled and unskilled manual occupations. However, 60% of unemployed workers are Catholics, Catholic unemployment rate is 25% compared to 11% for Protestants. For males the figures are 31% and 13%, and for those longer than two years unemployed the figures are 57% and 25%. A Catholic male between 18 and 25 years is two and a half times more likely to be unemployed than his Protestant counterpart.

Among the efforts to deal with unemployment are ACE schemes which tend to be limited to a year at a time, although there has been a new emphasis on training. Many of these are parish based and while the better ones provide a means of developing local lay leadership, in others there is a high degree of centralisation which tends to sap local initiative.

The medium term prospect is as bleak for those currently unemployed, in insecure jobs or planning to enter the labour force over the next few years. The net gain in private sector jobs is not likely to be more than 2,000 while the growth in the labour force due to natural increase will amount to 8,000.

To reduce Northern Ireland rates of unemployment to

UK rates even at a time of high unemployment in Great Britain would require a period of growth sustained over years at rates far in excess of the best that has been achieved at any time since the war. And this too at a time when large-scale international investments are few and far between, tending increasingly to go to low labour cost economies in developing countries and the Pacific rim, when public sector employment, on which Northern Ireland has been inordinately dependent, is contracting, and when the balance of employment generally is changing to short-term, part-time contracting out.

These conditions are likely to put a premium on skill and mobility for young people. The outbreak of peace in Northern Ireland could have an important role in stimulating the economy (balanced ironically by the loss of jobs and security). The impact of Europe post-1992 is also incalculable. One projection suggests that rationalisation of European economies will result in substantial job losses. On the other hand, Ireland, north and south, has a potential labour force which is young and intelligent. The question arises whether the work will come to Ireland or Irish people must travel to the European mainland to work – probably a bit of both – and whether attitudes to migration and emigration will change in the wider, more integrated European community. One thing is certain, emigration at best would be a matter of choice, but whether forced or free the potential emigrant will fare better with skills, training and preparation for the wider world.

What is clear too is that there will be a premium on skills and the ability to adapt. Increasingly people will not have a job for life and must be adaptable enough for three or more career changes in the course of a working life. There is also likely to be an increasing move towards self-employment and the development of an enterprise culture.

FAMILY VALUES

Perhaps a key area of social policy and pastoral responsibility is the family. Current British social policy, which is supposed to reflect traditional Tory values, stresses the importance of the family. There is often a distance between rhetoric and reality and many policies, especially the arrangements for social welfare are actually destructive of family cohesiveness. There are other structural changes too – increasing mobility tends to remove young people from their parents and this will increase. The hold of the extended family is weakening and this has implications for social care. In addition, the nature of the family is changing and not only in size. The number of one-parent families has increased markedly and there is significant coincidence between one-parent families and many forms of disadvantage and deprivation. There are indications too of greater and more realistic acceptance of marriage breakdown even of divorce and remarriage and of relatively stable relationships among young people which do not involve marriage.

A recent survey of the family by an Australian anthropologist (commissioned as a piece of market research by food retailers) found increasing anxiety about the structure and nature of the family. Most people saw the family as the most important thing in their lives but threatened by the struggle for economic survival, decline in living standards, rising crime rates and individualism. Underpinning the expectation that families would continue to live together were expectations that children would not be able to afford to own their own homes, that external entertainment would be increasingly costly and that the home is a security blanket against an increasingly hostile world. As a result, home will retain a social importance, but not in the form of a return to family activities. More typically it will mean a group of individuals each doing their own thing in separate rooms at separate times – the nuclear family having become atomised. As traditional family activities break down new groupings will emerge, more tribal in nature and based more on common interest than immediate blood ties. Work, clubs, hobbies and political groups will take the place of the spouse and children as a focus of individual interest.

While it is dangerous to transplant examples from one culture to another it is equally dangerous to believe that family has not changed and is not changing.

COMMUNITY VALUES

Equally one needs to ask what is happening to community and to society in an era when the dominant economic doctrine is market forces. Market forces may be an important motor to the economy but they are essentially dispassionate and involve winners and losers. They thrive on the creation of difference and on competition whereas the essential values of community are non-competitive and the removal, elision or softening of difference.

Increasingly one sees the emergence of two societies side by side which is characterised by the fact that in Northern Ireland at the same time there is the highest rate of dependency on social benefits in the United Kingdom and the highest sale of BMW cars. I believe that the same division is apparent in Dublin, in many ways a more unequal society. There is increasingly a division between those who are educated, skilled, mobile and in work and those who are unskilled, immobile, unemployed – and poor. Increasingly one sees whole communities where unemployment is endemic, where people are marginalised, impoverished and powerless. These are the people too who bear the great brunt both of urban crime and paramilitary activity, and the reactive pressures of constant policing and security activity.

Northern Ireland tends to be a conservative society but again with changes at the edges. Church attendances is high among both groups with Catholics twice as likely as Protestants to go to church once a week. Even among Catholics there is some indications of a decline but marginally from 90% to 80% over recent years (which is still very high by comparative European standards) and some anecdotal evidence of less regular attendances by young people in the inner city.

Both communities share an extremely conservative

moral attitude: there are strong feelings against pre-marital sex in both communities but a difference between age-groups: 18-34 are on average four times more permissive, although adultery is generally seen to be wrong by all age-groups (91% overall). So too were (82%) homosexual relationships although again the 18-34 age group were 20% more acceptive than those over 55. Northern Ireland people too are far from tolerant about AIDS. Four people out of ten thought AIDS to be a form of punishment for moral decadence and 57% though AIDS sufferers had only themselves to blame.

Against this conservative back-drop it is perhaps surprising that illegitimacy and teenage pregnancies increased by 70% in five years, that the number of births to teenage unmarried mothers increased from 54% in 1985 to 73% in 1989 (Eastern Health and Social Services Board area 83%) bringing with it an increase in the rate of peri-natal mortality. Then too there are the number of women from Ireland with Irish addresses going to England for abortions in the National Health Service – 1,816 from Northern Ireland and 3,721 from the Republic. These figures must represent an understatement of the real position and they are cloaked too by the ability of those with money and know-how to avoid becoming statistics. It may be another case, along with the number of young Irish people in prison, in care or on the streets of London, of Ireland exporting its social problems .

The question then arises is whether given the fall in fertility rates (in a society where the primary morality rejects contraception) the number of illegitimate pregnancies, the number of abortions represent a generally freer attitude among young people to sexual morality and whether there is a disparity between what people profess (or are regarded as professing) and their practice.

What I draw from this is a picture of a society which is divided to a marked degree between 75% who are doing all right (including some who are doing very well indeed) and the 25% who are not. Increasingly society is falling into two groups – those who are educated, skilled, mobile, in work, and relatively well-off and those who are unskilled, without work, immobile and poor. These latter are increasingly likely to be trapped in the inner city and as society becomes more competitive and less compassionate to be seen as having lost out in the race. In America there is talk of an urban underclass which is increasingly marginalised – kept out from the benefits of the wider society in requiring only subsistence report and pacification. This is a challenge facing society and the Churches in Ireland.

Rural Society

Colm Kilcoyne

They talk about three kinds of rural Ireland. The first two are regions close to large cities and regions which, though they are on the decline, still have good resources.

Thirdly, there are regions which are isolated, with poor land, small holdings, underdeveloped infrastructure. These are regions where what is at stake is not simply the profit margin but the very survival of families and communities.

The land in this kind of rural region was generally poor to begin with but now there is every chance that it will be simply abandoned and revert to a kind of desert.

This is John Healy's snipe grass country. It is the Hungry Grass of the *Mayo Book of Theology*.

It is the rural Ireland I am most familiar with. On the principle that you should only talk about what you both know and care about I confine myself to this, third, region of rural Ireland.

One thing about this third kind of rural Ireland: you have to dig deeper, throw back more scraw, to discover traces of a divided society. You'll certainly find rich and poor in this rural Ireland, but not as starkly opposed as in urban Ireland – and not obscene enough to say: It is because of this we can call this a divided society.

Neither do you get the tension of cultures that you get in the North – at least not on the scale that would let you say: It is because of this we can call this a divided society.

You certainly have secularisation, of the kind Liam Ryan spoke about – but, again, not profound enough to say: It is because of this we can call this a divided society.

There is a deceptive sameness about my rural Ireland.

The pot-holes at one end of any parish are pretty much the same as those at the other end. Indeed, they have a depressing sameness across all rural dioceses – despite the occasional boast of Kilmore diocese that their's is a superior class of pot hole. No clue to divisions there.

Housing is no great help, either. It looks good and standard. A legacy from the 1970s when we began to milk the EEC cow with one hand and draw wages from the multinationals with the other.

In my home town of Castlebar, Travenol. a health-care multinational, employed 750 workers, mainly couples They commuted from a radius of maybe twenty, thirty miles. His wage fed and clothed them. Hers paid the mortgage. And the creamery cheque went back to the bank to pay for land developments. No clue to divisions there.

Schools. I suggest the quality of rural schools varies according to the energy of the Board of Management, rather than according to local incomes. Post-primary schools are uniformly good. No clue to divisions there.

As for the people of rural Ireland: well, them what knows tell us we have a grey sameness – conservative, dole-dependent, fatalistic and sulkily obedient to the Church. They tell us we are a people cursed with a hard memory. A dark people. Clod-conceived. Burdened with a famine mentality. Reared on hungry grass that gets hungrier by the day.

Poor soil, you'd imagine, for any kind of news, good, bad or indifferent.

And yet, this is the soil, these are the people, who responded so magnificently, so enthusiastically, in the seventies, to the Good News of the Economic Prophets.

THE BEST OF TIMES ...

In a matter of years, months in some cases, these people shed the gloom of history and set out after the prophets, for the Promised Land. We hitched our wagon to the EEC cow, and for some years, the land did flow with milk and honey. We drained it, we smothered it with fertilisers, we did all that the prophets told us do. We built our bungalows and turned the old homes into outhouses.

Around the same time, the multinationals discovered the delights of rural labour. In Castlebar, Travenol – 750 workers. In Killala, Asahi – 350 workers In Ballina, Hollister – 400 workers In Westport, Allergan – 250 workers In Ballyhaunis, Halal – Allah alone knows how many, but a lot.

It was big stuff and signs on Mayo, it was flying. Our prosperity was supported by a three-legged stool. One leg was EEC money, another was the multinational wage, the third was our land.

The prophets of economic Good News told us the first two legs were sound and that in time they'd strengthen the third. It was looking good.

So what if the spin-off jobs were few. They reckon that in Mayo there were three printing works that could point to an extra twenty-nine workers between them as a result of business from the county-based multinationals. One precision engineering firm said it took just two workers to handle multinational orders. Only 11% of the materials used in those Mayo factories was sourced in Mayo. Only 15% came from anywhere else in Ireland. The other 85% was imported. Of course, there were wages and services.

But it was a shaky leg. Once the grants had run their term, or corporate headquarters in downtown Biloxi got a chill, the virus sped to downtown Bohola in days.

Still, we had two sound legs and a bit of juggling gave us a bit of stability.

Now, the other leg. the EEC one, is wobbling. Brussels is fussing and making noises about GATT and CAP. And what is simply breath-taking is that the same kind of prophet who stalked the land in the '70s and proclaimed the Good News of Plenty with such confidence, is at it again – this time preaching disaster with equal confidence.

And now, people in rural Ireland are asking the obvious of the experts. How did all this happen? Were you working out of a vision or making it up as you went along? Can we trust you now? Does anybody real know anything about anything?

With these questions comes a depression. Those of you who work in the kind of rural Ireland I'm talking about have sensed this depression. It is part of a chain of communal bereavement. And it has all the classic stages of bereavement. Anger now. Then acceptance. And back to anger and depression again.

It is in the songs of the Sawdoctors and goes a long way to explain the massive identity the west has with their lyrics, with the angry, angular touching sound of their music and their general irreverence for institutions.

Parents feel defeated. Parents who thought they'd seen the back of emigration now feel they see the end of the line with no one staying for the place. No place worth staying for. No one to hand it over to. Nothing worth handing over.

AT ODDS WITH OURSELVES

Now, I think, we've turned back the scraw enough to reveal the division in rural society. It is the terrible separation of a people from their aspirations.

A rural society collectively separated from continuity between past and future.

An embarrassed society that lost control to men without vision. Disenfranchised with promises. Led astray by false prophets.

There is a sense of violation, of having lost some integrity. A bright, educated people who bought into a dream sold them by others who said, 'Trust us and sign here.' They did and now they are at odds with themselves.

Twelve rural communities in the west were surveyed by your own western region of the NCPI. The profiles of these communities were interchangeable, showing distrust of bureaucrats and politicians. Depression. Emigration.

10% of the population have emigrated from these western regions since 1985. An awful haemorrhage if you scale it down to one in ten in an average village – and if that one in ten is educated and young.

In the west, since 1985, one in three school leavers lives locally, one in three lives elsewhere in Ireland and one in three has gone abroad.

Three times the population of Ballinrobe has left Tuam diocese in the last five years. Half a million have left Ireland since 1980. Talk about a divided society.

On a mantelpiece in Mayo the other day I saw envelopes from Germany, Boston, New York, and London. All from family. Divided family. You can say all you want about the positive side of this but it still adds up to a lot of heartache, a lot of disorientated people, a lot of uncertainty about the future.

Who can say what is happening to young people who grow up and get educated in one culture, with the certain knowledge that they will finish up in another culture, almost certainly doing work that doesn't come within an ass's roar of either their aspirations or their qualifications.

Emigration doesn't just take away the bright: it debilitates those left behind.

There is now a malaise in rural Ireland. Low income

matched by low morale. The welfare dependency is un-
healthy, the infrastructure unserviced.

FEEDING CYNICISM

Things happen that make rural people cynical. A meeting of
EEC officials in Ashford Castle in Mayo meant all the roads
they'd travel on were repaired. The roads the locals use
every day were left untouched.

In the same area Galway County Council brought in a
£70,000 machine to fill in pot holes with limestone chips
brought up from Limerick. Now, this is a limestone area itself. And the work used to be done by a few locals who
maintained the roads and, in the process, maintained their
own dignity.

A separation of people from their environment, an erosion of pride in place. There's a lovely phrase that the Jewish people used when they spoke to the Pope on his recent
visit to Hungary. They were talking about their anger at the
memory of the Hungarian Holocaust, especially since they
had given Hungary loyalty. They said they had always
abided by the wisdom of their old Jewish saying: Work for
the peace of the place where you live, for this shall be your
peace.

Many people in rural Ireland lack peace, for that reason.

GOSPEL

Okay. Where does the real Good News fit into this? How
can it take root where so much cockle has been sown in two

decades? How preach it to a demoralised people? What language to use, what symbols?

Simple things first. There can be no harm in looking at how Jesus Christ did it. His first point of contact with people who were separated from themselves was an attitudinal thing. He showed he cared for them, he showed they counted as individuals.

This is a profound truth about human relationships, not simply a communications trick or a salesman's ploy. We appreciate it when we experience it from those with leadership roles in our lives. So, too do parishoners. It is the essential first step.

It will matter if we care and people know they count.

There's a phrase at home, 'How's the care?' How are those closest to your heart? How do you love those who share your heart blood?

Families pull through crises when there is care. So will Christian communities.

Every time a priest does something selfless, he patches the vision for people. Every time someone gets the experience of being cared for, that parishioner is rebaptized.

That matters. Because it gives hope and releases gifts. Hidden energies are recognised and given their head in a community where people feel their baptismal dignity.

The Sunday Eucharist plays a vital function in this ministry of care and dignity.

I have pity on these people for they have been with me for three days and now have nothing to eat. I don't want to send them away without feeding them for they might faint on the way.

There is a strength, nowadays, in rural Ireland, as seeing the Sunday Eucharist as bread for the journey.

That's the heart response - the attitudinal thing.

The head. For our part, mustn't we inform ourselves not just of the facts about rural decline but of the consequences? I know that rural development seminars have become a new growth industry but we need them. We need them to know what is happening, what will happen.

The head again. I think we need to be more aware of the new consciousness among women. I'm not just talking about women and the Church. I'm not talking about women who go to seminars on the role of women. I'm talking about a general awareness born of better education and an articulacy about emotions and values that would leave us standing.

This new consciousness will dictate how faith is handed on in the homes. I have no worries about it – only about how we priests respond to it.

The heart. The head. The hand. There is the occasional James Horan and James McDyer. Builders. Self starters. Entrepreneurs. It was said of James Horan: Where two or three blocks are gathered together, there is James in the midst of them – planning to build a wall.

For the rest of us, our talent probably lies more in encouraging others to find blocks, others again who will bring the blocks to the one spot and others again who will build a wall. They now call this empowering people. A good phrase because it has a truth behind it. It will coax talents out of the shy shadows. It will help people analyse projects more honestly. It will bring back into synch. people's feelings about themselves and their place.

So, in summary, I'm saying that rural Ireland is a divided society in that the people are separated from their vision. The Good News in society takes the form of hope for the heart, a rediscovery of human and baptismal dignity for the head, and as a result, a release of hidden energies for their hands.

Community Development and the Role of the Priest

Mary Whelan

What I have been asked to do is to locate what I have to say within my own experience of living and working in Ireland and particularly, within my experience of working in community development over the last twenty years. So I will say who I am and the context I speak from.

I grew up in Roscommon in the '40s and '50s. We weren't poor, but I saw plenty of rural poverty. Emigration was the safety valve and most people lived on what I discovered afterwards were called 'emigrants' remittances'. I went to secondary school to Dublin, to the civil service and the corporation and eventually to the United States in the '60s to train as a social worker.

I was in Alabama in 1964 and the Civil Rights Movement shattered my political naivete and deeply affected me. The American war on poverty which gave way to the war in Vietnam introduced me to ideas like citizen participation and community organisation. I went to the United States to learn how to help people with their problems as a social worker. I came home asking why these problems existed in the first place and with a deep belief that people could and should change their political reality and that there could be change and justice.

I walked straight into the 1971 Poverty Conference in Kilkenny. Organised by the Catholic bishops, it opened Irish eyes to the huge problem of poverty in the country and documented it beyond doubt. I saw hope that we were waking up and gave up social work for community development.

TRADITION OF COMMUNITY DEVELOPMENT

In Ireland, we have a long tradition of community development going back to Canon Hayes and the foundation of Muintir na Tíre. Its emphasis on participation and collective action by ordinary people seemed to me to provide a way of tackling poverty and deprivation where they were most keenly felt and also a way of getting resources to do so. From a community development perspective, people were mobilising for participation in the '60s and early '70s. The women's movement was beginning in Ireland, a huge number of community councils and community-based self-help groups were set up, a strong tenant movement and a housing action movement emerged in some areas, especially in Dublin. Places like Glencolumbkille and West Connemara and bodies such as the Rural Housing Organisation were becoming symbols of hope in rural areas.

In 1974, an Anti-Poverty Programme which was largely instigated by the Irish government was set up in member states of the EC. The Irish programme, which had an important effect on community development practice here, defined poverty in structural terms and drew attention to the fact that the eventual elimination of poverty would require the redistribution of resources and power in society. This implied the need for basic changes in the socio-economic and political systems and it was an analysis which was not favourably received by the government. The concept of local people organising to bring about change which was central to the way the programme was run here, was seen as an unacceptable challenge to the established power structures. By 1980 when the poverty programme was closed down without its lessons being heard, much less implemented, things had begun to change. At local level the results of economic recession and rising unemployment meant a change in the role of many community groups.

During the '80s, a wide variety of State schemes was introduced in response to unemployment and the increasing marginalisation of disadvantaged areas. None of them dealt with the causes of marginalisation, but all of them depended on community groups to implement them. The result is that, for example, temporary employment schemes, temporary training schemes and enterprise development schemes are now being run by local groups which rely on State sponsorship. Some groups which were set up originally to develop participation and organise campaigns on issues like housing, unemployment and urban renewal, have become fully occupied administering State schemes. Small local groups in communities with 70% unemployment are finding themselves discussing partnerships with the State and private sectors under various national and EC initiatives, partnerships where they are the junior and powerless partner and where, sometimes, the responsibility even to create their own jobs is being transferred from the government to the shoulders of people who suffer the consequences of unjust and unequal policies at national and international level.

However, when a quarter of a million people are out of work, community groups are caught up in the survival struggle of poor communities. They cannot be blamed for accepting State sponsorship and administering the pittances people get paid on temporary schemes even though they are very well aware that this is not the solution that is needed.

ROLE OF THE PRIEST

So where is the Church in these new partnerships which are supposed to bring about change? I feel that the Church as an institution is a 'sleeping partner' which has not declared what side it is on. But I do not believe that that is true of many sisters and priests with whom I have worked in local communities, whose commitment to change and justice is total and who are often themselves unsupported by the church to which they belong. My experience is local and I am going to confine these brief few words to the priest in the local community, in the context of what I have been saying up to now.

Firstly, I believe that the priest has power. People say that is changing and I know that church attendance has decreased dramatically in some communities and local people no longer automatically accept the traditional leadership role of the priest. But what has not changed, in my view, is the central role he occupies when it comes to negotiations with statutory bodies and the advantages of parish sponsorship and support for groups struggling to get resources.

Example. I was working with a group which had spent a year campaigning and getting its act together on an issue of vital local importance. We had produced a report and finally got the ear of a senior politician who agreed to meet us. We felt a lot depended on the meeting. He was in a position to make decisions. We had to convince him.

We prepared: everyone had their bit to say, the local angle, research that had been done, people's right to resources. Eight of us went in, including a local priest who was a member of the group and was very involved locally. The woman who was chairperson of the group spoke first, explained the background to why we were there, the work we had done, the urgent need for action in this community and what we were hoping would come out of the meeting. When she had finished, the politician turned to her, smiled at her, looked across the table at the priest and said: 'Now, Father, will you tell me why you are here?' We wondered if he would have done the same if a man had been chairperson of the group?

This power, and it is power which a priest has, can be used to perpetuate the collusion between church and state which ends up keeping people out and dis-empowering them or it can be used to share power or transfer power to local people so that they can learn to run their own affairs without intermediaries. I might add here that many of the points I am making in relation to the priest in the community are applicable also to other professionals, and especially to community workers like myself. We have the choice often of running things *for* people or having the basic respect and trust to enable people to run things for themselves.

RESEARCH

In our organisation, Community Action Network, we have recently carried out a study of six community development projects in Dublin. They are well established projects, located in disadvantaged areas, struggling to implement community development principles. In five of the six projects, we found that sisters and priests played important roles.

There were three different ways in which they were involved. In two, the priests involved had leadership roles based on their formal positions as local parish priests. They negotiated State funding and set up community development projects in the area.

In two more projects the priests involved had no formal position in the area, they lived as tenants in flats there and they facilitated and supported local development work. They tried to build confidence locally and used their access to outside contacts to benefit the community.

In the fifth project, two sisters were employed by the diocese to develop a community-based response to problems associated with poverty and unemployment in a newly developing area.

The sixth project we studied had no religious involvement, but was seriously aggrieved when another local project, which was Church sponsored, got substantial State funding which it could not get. They saw this as an example of the clear advantages of Church sponsorship when it comes to negotiations with the State. Especially, they saw Church-sponsored projects as having advantages over a local group, as they are, which has constantly tried to point out the political causes of poverty and disadvantage.

This study illustrated the important role of the Church in community-based work. It was not something we set out to study, it emerged in the course of looking at the origins and work of the projects.

The study showed more recent approaches, where priests and sisters live in communities and facilitate people to develop themselves rather than play a leadership role. It also showed, however, that ordinary parish structures can promote empowerment and local control, where this is built in to the approach taken by the priest.

For example, in one community, an education and training project was initiated by a parish priest and got substantial State funding. As soon as the money came through and the project was set up, he withdrew from management and decision-making in it. Nine of its thirteen-member management group were local people. It now functions as a locally controlled project which has developed its own relationship with parish structures. Parishes who operate in this way have had to face up to issues of control or development. They have to decide whether they are going to put their resources, contacts and status at the disposal of local people, whether they are going to trust people to run their lives and support them to do so, or whether they need to put a Church stamp on what they do and thereby prevent it belonging to the people it is all about in the first place.

A friend of mine in the inner city always says: 'We'll still be here when you have all gone on to other things'. The priest who set up the project I just mentioned has moved on. But he has left something which belongs to the people of the community he passed through.

EMPOWERING THE LOCAL PEOPLE

To conclude: I know I have been talking about the local parish and not 'the Church'. That is because I can see the local parish; I can feel its dynamics; I can go to its meetings. There is a need for huge changes in Church policy. If there is a heave at local level, maybe these will happen. Maybe the power and influence of the Church would move in behind people who are marginalised if the demand came from the ground.

The constituents of every priest are the people he works with every day, not the bishops. It is the local people who need empowering, not the people who have the power already. Everyone says we lack leadership. I am not waiting for a great leader; not a bishop; certainly not a pope.

Leadership to me is showing what side you are on, taking a stand, allowing your sense of outrage at injustice to find expression, even when it is unpopular or regarded as an emotional outburst. Leadership is standing back and supporting other people to become leaders in their own community. Leadership is not colluding with the State in putting a 'safe' stamp on initiatives which should challenge unjust structures.

People who have most inspired me are those who go through the hard slog of development work on the ground and who have faced up to issues about the meaning of development in the day-to-day struggle for justice.

The Rich and the Poor

Raymond Murray

Admed Kassim

Jesus did not redeem the world out of nothing;
he redeemed it out of a little boy's satchel,
that day in the desert
when he fed the five thousand
with five barley loaves and two fish,
all that the youngster had.
The boy was reluctant to part with them.
His mother had prepared his lunch
at daybreak,
kissed his forehead
and bade him farewell.
Jesus did not throw a feast out of nothing,
he multiplied the boy's generosity.
The child emptied his bundle,
gave up his meal to be fed on words.
Jesus learned his first lesson.

On the fourth day of February
nineteen hundred and ninety one,
Black Crows gathered in the heavens without fear,

the Allies from the Western World.
They quickly unburdened their gigantic sacks,
and destroyed a bridge in southern Iraq.
They killed the people fleeing from al-Nasiriyeh.

It was Jesus who recognised Adhmed Kassim,
the boy with the loaves,
lying on a stretcher,
still wearing the red cardigan his mother had knit for him
so skilfully without a seam,
his head crowned with shrapnel thorns,
holes in his feet, a wound in his side.
He was only ten years of age.
Jesus learned his second lesson.

That is a translation of a poem in Irish I published in *An tUl-tach*. If you think it isn't good I can say it suffered in translation!

Propaganda called the Gulf War a clean war, a surgical operation, but here was killing comparable to Hiroshima and Dresden, a re-enactment of 'Bomber' Harris's aerial murder raid on Lübeck on 28 March 1942. Abrams tanks of the First Mechanised Infantry Division equipped with bull-dozer blades drove parallel to Iraqi trenches and buried soldiers alive. The Basra road carnage of fleeing helpless soldiers reminded one of the worst features of the First World War. The systematic destruction of the civil infrastructure of Iraq has led to the ill-health of millions of people and a high rate of infant mortality. The allies sought to destroy *en masse* the Iraqi forces in Kuwait and south-eastern Iraq. These were mainly peasant conscripts and reservists. Their surrender would have been a matter of course but the allies chose to treat them as 'target rich'. Thousands of fuel-air explosives and slurry bombs and cluster bombs which spill out hundreds of grenades, and missiles from the Multiple Rocket Launch System (MRLS) poured down on the unfortunates. There is little sympathy in western Europe and in the United States of America for the victims. Governments of western Europe and the USA deliberately deny their peoples access to the culture of the Arabs. Pope John Paul stood almost isolated in his condemnation of the Gulf War. The disciples of the Lord fled as at Gethsemane.

I welcome my inheritance of western culture. I hope I am positive about accepting the benefits of modern technology. I do not, however, accept as utopia the ideology of secular liberalism, pluralism or a 'democracy' based on capitalism. The *Brandt Report*, which exposes the North-South divide of the earth, is too much a reproach for that. History repeats itself. Empires rise and fall. Each great new power regards itself as 'civilisation' and frowns on the rest of the world as 'barbarism'. New Caesars need not lop off the enemy tribe's right hands. They can bury them alive in trenches. The Rockeye II, weighing about five hundred pounds, dispenses 247 grenade-sized bomblets which produce a hail of around half a million anti-personnel shrapnel fragments which can kill or severely wound anyone within an acre. All that is needed is a target-rich area of human beings.

I believe there is a utopia or a *parousia* – the redemption of Jesus Christ. That demands moving into the world of spirit. Redemption, like creation, is an on-going thing. People in every age are heroic in their suffering, sacrifice and generosity. Jesus is eternally alive and he learns from every age of humanity. The boy with the loaves in the desert and Adhmed Kassim are telescoped.

ON THE WRONG SIDE OF THE TRACK ...

I do not find the Northern Ireland problem difficult to understand. It is in microcosm the problem of many countries and states in the world. The division of Rich and Poor is the basis of the division in Northern Ireland. Discrimination against Catholics was administrative policy of the Stormont Government for fifty years. Its rule lacked charity and justice. In that sense the war in the north is a religious war. The facts of this injustice were admitted publicly by the British Government in the Cameron Report on Disturbances in Northern Ireland of 1969. Justice in the work places is still being pursued by the Fair Employment Agency in Northern Ireland and by Irish people armed with the McBride Principles who lobby institutions of power in the USA. Sharing, power-sharing, is an answer to the Northern Ireland problem. The British Government has further aggravated the dominance of one community and culture over the other by the one-sided structuring of the Royal Ulster Constabulary and the Ulster Defence Regiment which places security and power solely in the hands of Unionists. This serious mistake has led to corruption of law, harassment, state killings and collusion of government forces with loyalist paramilitaries.

The ghetto people of Northern Ireland, particularly those in Derry and West Belfast, are like other ghetto people. They regard themselves, in John Steinbeck's phrase, as on 'the wrong side of the track'. Problems like vandalism, illiteracy, drugs, and violence in ghetto cities are basically the result of deprivation. There is a temptation on the part of government to regard these problems as a matter of 'law and order'. That embitters the situation. The 'haves' and 'have nots' divide seems to be perennial. It has led to major conflicts in today's world – South Africa, Nicaragua, El Salvador, the Philippines.

The Rich eventually are forced to take notice of the situation. What do they say to the Poor? They dictate to them from government offices, palaces, penthouse flats and mansions. The more they dictate to them, the more the Poor resent their solutions. They presume the loyalty of the ghettos to the State but many ghetto people hate the State. Sometimes the Poor reply with bombs and guns, as much as to say, 'Well, if I don't share, you are not going to enjoy your wealth in peace'. That is the *raison d'être* of anarchy.

Why, for example, should the Northern Ireland Office presume the loyalty of the people of Ballymurphy, a little housing estate of nationalists in Belfast where in the past twenty years over sixty people have been shot dead by security forces and loyalist gangs, where houses on numerous occasions have been systematically wrecked by police and soldiers, where nearly every able-bodied man has been interned or imprisoned? Who built that ugly ghetto in the first place?

LISTENING TO THE POOR

Liberation theology has something relevant to say to us here. It can be summed up in the phrase 'Listen to the Poor'. The Rich have an attitude: 'Can anything good come out of Nazareth'? Can anything good come out of Ballymurphy? Can anything good come out of Ballyfermot? The Poor want no plan handed down to them, neither from the USA Government, nor from the Northern Ireland Office, nor from Leinster House, nor from the Irish Episcopal Conference, nor from the National Conference of Priests of Ireland, nor from the International Funds. What are the Poor saying themselves? Come down and listen to them. They don't want people telling them, 'What you want is ... '

Northern Ireland mirrors the world-wide problem of the Rich and the Poor, the resource-hungry northern hemisphere devouring the southern. If oil or any other aspect of the economy is a problem then the powerful, in the name of democracy and the free world, will bury the weak with great earth-movers. The creed of secular liberalism, materialism and capitalism provides the philosophy to do so.

Secularism can be a pseudo moral voice that offers us more and more to eat and drink, comforts us with blockbuster bestsellers with sex and violence on every page, assassinates the characters of other moral voices in competition and shields the sins of media bosses. It wrecks the unity of the family and aborts children from the womb. Its bland monotonous sameness provokes the revolt of the small nations and cultures anxious to preserve their national heritages. It threatens non-conformists with nuclear and chemical weapons and aspires to Star Wars.

But what about the enemy within? Could it be that as the ghettos expand in this brave new world we will live to see the Poor rise again in a new socialist revolution? Who says socialism is dead?

Where does the world of the sacred stand confronted by the pervasive dominance of this heady secularism? Does it respond by tirelessly proclaiming the old virtues – disciplined prayer, disciplined charity, disciplined chastity, conservative authority?

Or will the sacred try to survive in dialogue with the secular and content itself with small committed Christian communities, bright faith globules in the darkening pagan sea?

Priests in the field have no time to answer. Every day a desert boy hands them a satchel of bread and fish. Every day they find Adhmed Kassim lying wounded on a stretcher. Like Jesus they have learned their lesson.

The Gospel in Irish Society

Donal Dorr

My topic is 'The Gospel in Irish Society'. Before addressing the topic I must first address, you, the people to whom I am speaking, and take some account of who you are. For most of you, your life is defined largely by the fact that you are priests - ministers and functionaries of the Catholic Church. Your lives are so deeply bound up with the Church that the burning issue here is what the Church should be doing about the issues that came up in the other papers and what you should be doing as priests and representatives of the Church.

But you and I are not defined solely as ministers of the Church. Before being Church functionaries we are human beings, we are committed Christians, and most of us are ministerial by temperament and calling. (That becomes obvious when one of us leaves the official priesthood: he nearly always gets involved in some other form of ministry.)

So I address you now mainly as humans, as people of the Gospel and as people with a sense of being called to minister to those around you and to the wider Irish society – and perhaps also to the global society and to the earth itself.

I ask you to put on the back boiler for the next half-hour your pressing concerns about the Church and your role in it and to broaden your horizon to see yourself first as a minister of the Gospel rather than of the Church.

I have a number of reasons for emphasising the Gospel rather than the Church. One is that the Church in Ireland is an integral part of the whole set of problems that were explored in other papers. So we need to disengage somewhat from the Church and evaluate its role in the light of the Gospel.

A second reason for stressing the Gospel is the rapidly changing perception of the priest in society. Up to very recent times, our priesthood gave us great moral authority. When we spoke or acted as priests we had a lot of credibility with most people in Ireland, whereas in Britain the Anglican clergyman was not taken very seriously.

In today's Ireland priests still have considerable moral authority among some sectors of society while in other sectors the fact that we are priests gives us a negative credibility rather than adding to our credibility.

I want to note three such sectors in particular:

First, there is a very significant number of women (mainly younger and more educated women) who are alienated from the Catholic Church. It is an understatement to say that these women do not feel heard by the Church and do not feel the Church is taking account of, or speaking to, their deepest concerns. I remember hearing a deeply religious woman say, 'I have stopped going to Mass because I could no longer endure being assaulted by what the priests were saying and doing there.' It was obvious in the group that she had put words on the feelings of several other women.

Secondly, there is a growing segment of the urbanized working-class both in Northern Ireland and in the South who are now either alienated from the Church or positively hostile to it. When I say 'working-class' I do not mean they are workers; in fact very many of these people are chronically unemployed, while many of the working-class people who are still in regular employment have remained faithful Church-people.

Thirdly, there is an important segment of middle-class people, mainly 'yuppie' people involved in business; they may be liberal or conservative on political or sexual issues, but what defines them is that they are 'economic liberals'. Their attitude to the Church is quite similar to that of the economic liberals of the last century: they want it, but only on their own terms. They like the Church to be there as a support to the political and economic *status quo* and perhaps to provide good schools for their children. But they have not the slightest interest in the social teaching of the Church. And when the Church takes a stand on issues of justice and poverty these people are either angry or totally dismissive.

Between them these three sectors of society cover a large and growing proportion of the total population. So, unless there is a major change in the approach of the Church, it is unlikely in the coming years to have any big impact on society.

Nevertheless I do not think it is a waste of time for us to reflect together here on the Gospel and society. For if we discover the relevance of the Gospel to our world then we may be accepted as human beings and as ministers by the alienated women and the alienated working-class not because we are representatives of the Church but in spite of it. This in turn may enable us to find both the inspiration and energy to bring about some major changes in the Church itself. So, although I am speaking to you as ministers of the Gospel rather than Church functionaries, what I am saying has implications for the role of the Church in our society, and for your role as ministers of the Church.

THE GOSPEL TODAY

What the Gospel is saying to today's world is that God wants ordinary people to be free at every level:
- free in the depth of their hearts and spirit;
- free and open in their relationships with others,
- free from the exploitation, hunger and oppression to which our present kind of society condemns most people in the Third World;
- free from the drudgery or joblessness which is the lot of the poor in our own country;
- free from the emptiness, alienation and meaninglessness which our society evokes in many better-off people.

The Gospel is also saying that where we find God above all is precisely in our struggle to gain these freedoms and to accept them and live them out in our daily lives.

To the ordinary people of his own time Jesus offered real freedom of spirit. He invited them to get out from under the religious tyranny of scribes and pharisees who claimed that

God accepts only those who enslave themselves to elaborate legalism and ritualism. Many people in the Irish situation today are hungry for the same freedom of spirit – a rescue from a legalistic, moralistic, clericalist and almost superstitious conception of Christianity. As ministers we cannot give them such freedom, but we can refuse absolutely to collude in anything that fosters or panders to such notions.

Then we can go on to facilitate people in working towards true freedom of spirit; and we can give affirmation and encouragement to those who have the courage to accept it. In doing so we shall be helping not only those who are trapped in legalism but also those who have rejected Christian faith or practice precisely because they experience it as legalistic or superstitious rather than as promoting real freedom of spirit.

In this way we open up to people the possibility of finding God at the heart of their daily lives, especially in their struggle for inner and outer freedom. Looking at this from another point of view we can say that in helping people to discover true freedom we are making available the energy and inspiration of the Gospel, and the grace and power of God, to those who are weighed down by the daily struggle for freedom and authenticity.

We begin with two key issues, namely, helping people to find God and helping them to live a fully human life in society. In the long run these turn out to be really the same: to find how to live an authentically human life is to find God. However, that convergence is what defines the end of our exploration; we have to begin with two different starting points.

FINDING GOD

As a Christian I believe that God is waiting for us at all times and in all places. That is what I take from the Gospel story of Jesus' meeting with the Samaritan women (Jn 4:21-3). The time has come when God and religious experience is not confined to the holy places of Samaria or Jerusalem or Mecca or Rome or Medjugorje. Religious leaders cannot control access to God; for God is present to all who are present to themselves in spirit and truth.

Nevertheless, the entry point to religious experience is very much an *à la carte* affair. For God offers us a whole menu of different kinds of peak experience where people may become present to themselves in spirit and in truth – situations where people feel lifted above the everyday grind to come in touch with the transcendent dimension of their lives. For many people this takes place when they contemplate the beauty of nature, or the power of the ocean. Others experience it when they come in touch with the tenderness of sexual love. A lot of people find it in the mystery of new life as they rejoice in the birth of a longed-for child or find their heart pierced by the smile of an infant. Some of us find it in the experience of community when we celebrate together, or go on a march or a pilgrimage together. Others come in touch with their most authentic selves in making a costly decision about what they want to do with their lives or in choosing a lifestyle which is at odds with the accepted values of society.

Some of the peak experiences which open us up to our deepest spirit and to God's Spirit are not just personal or interpersonal but have a political and cultural character. In Irish history people often found both themselves and God in the struggle to overcome oppression and domination; and in recent years Latin American and South African Christians have a similar experience. For very many women today the most privileged peak experiences come in their personal and interpersonal exploration and celebration of what it really means to be a woman and in their cultural and political struggle to have that recognised by others. And for a growing number of people today the really special way to religious experience comes from a renewed relationship with the earth itself – allowing it to nourish us and seeking to protect it from destruction and exploitation.

All of these peak experiences are situations where we feel ourselves more fully human – and that is precisely why we can find God in them. For that is the core of the Good News of Jesus: that God is not somewhere 'up there' or 'out there' but is at the heart of our lives, most fully present to us when we are most fully human. The meaning of the incarnation is not simply that Jesus was both human and divine. It is rather that it was precisely in being fully and authentically human that he was divine. And furthermore that he was our model in this: our only way to come in touch with God is to become more authentically human.

I have been mentioning various items from the long menu offered us by God, a menu of 'starters' or *hors d'ouvres*, which can whet our appetite and open us up to find ourselves and God in all aspects of life. I want now to focus on one such experience which is particularly relevant to the situation in Ireland which is explored in earlier papers. It is the experience of moving from desperation to freedom. It occurs in two spheres of life – in the depth of the human spirit and in the public arena of politics, economics and culture. I want to look at each of them in turn in the light of the Gospel.

FROM DESPERATION TO FREEDOM OF SPIRIT

Many people today live lives of desperation, barely surviving from day to day. The causes are manifold and sometimes cumulative – having to face each new day with no hope of finding a job; finding oneself at the mercy of an uncaring bureaucracy; wives or children being victims of physical violence; women or children subject to on-going sexual abuse or harassment; chronic ill-health; addiction to drugs or alcohol; overcrowded and alienating living conditions, or having no home at all, or (for Travellers) being pushed out of one camp-site after another; a gnawing sense of emptiness and lack of human fulfilment in work and recreation; the absence of a support structure and of a sense of community; growing old in a society which fails to respect the elderly – the list goes on and on.

What does the Gospel have to say to those who find

themselves in such desperate straits? (That is a very different question from asking what does the Church say to them; for in the past the message from the Church was mainly to put up with it in the hope of reward in heaven and, at times, today what these desperate people hear from the Church is not very different.) In the Gospel, on the other hand, we find not words of comfort but the story of the agony of Jesus. We see him prostrated by utter desperation, facing death as a criminal and heretic, totally overwhelmed by primal terror.

His sweat of desperation is very important for us. For it shows that the incarnation was not a case of God dropping in to visit us but of Jesus taking on even this most awful part of the human situation. And he shows us the way forward. It is not a matter of trying to block out the desperation – to find an escape through drugs, alcohol or 'pie in the sky'. If he had refused to allow it into consciousness, he would have been blocking access to the deepest part of his spirit.

What Jesus did was to acknowledge the desperation but not to yield to it. He allowed it in, admitting to his friends that he felt weighed down 'unto death' (Mk 14:34). He asked for their support as he struggled to survive. For he felt totally swamped in desperation as he allowed in the full implications of the task to which he had committed himself and to which he had even looked forward with a burning desire (Lk 12:50).

As he began his prayer into the darkness Jesus did not pretend to be anything other than desperate; he cried out, 'take this chalice away from me'. Slowly he moved on from there and his struggle took most of the night. It was only after many hours that he could say: 'Arise, let us go.' (Mt 26:46). He had moved from desperation to freedom of spirit and had found the strength to face up with authenticity to the culmination of his life's work.

What the Gospel says is that even those who are in a totally desperate situation may find a way to freedom of spirit. In South Africa a friend told me an incident about the well-known Protestant Church leader Frank Chicane. A couple of years ago he was detained by the South African security forces. After some days of being tortured he was thrown back into his cell and he cried out to God: 'I cannot take it any more, you've just got to do something.' Next day they took him out and tortured him again. He staggered back and prayed the same prayer. No change; he was tortured again next day and afterwards he prayed to God: 'You remember that message I sent you yesterday? Well, that prayer is still there on my screen. Are you not reading me?' That touch of grim humour was already the beginnings of an answer to his prayer. For the person who can make even a feeble joke is no longer utterly desperate. The torture didn't stop for several days more, but his spirit had already triumphed over it from that moment onward.

I do not need to spell out for you how important it is for people in a desperate situation to know that they can find a way to freedom of spirit. And I do not intend to spend time suggesting ways in which you could help people to experience this for themselves – except, of course, to remind you that the most ineffective way is for you as a priest to come along and tell this to a desperate person. Your words won't help, but your silent presence might. But if you don't already know that from your own pastoral experience then my warning won't make any difference. I am only trying to put words on what you already know from your experience and in your deepest heart.

DESPERATION IN THE PUBLIC ARENA

If I were to stop at this point it would be dangerous, because it might imply that the only thing that really matters is the inner struggle for freedom of spirit. But I want to say that from a Gospel perspective this personal struggle must go hand in hand with a public struggle for human freedom and authentic human life. For the Christian belief is that Jesus came not just to save us out of the world but to save the world itself. And at present our world finds itself in a desperate situation.

I believe that many Irish priests are uneasy and dispirited because they sense that their ministry is either not addressing the desperate crisis of our society, or is doing so quite ineffectively. These priests find they have become Church civil servants or functionaries. They are so involved in serving the institutional Church that, on the one hand, they do not have the inner freedom to engage in the radically personal ministry we have been speaking of; and, on the other hand, they are not fully convinced of the validity or urgency of the public role played by the Church in Irish society.

At present a great deal of the energy of the Catholic Church in Ireland is devoted to the task of preserving what is called 'the Catholic ethos' in schools, hospitals and the other institutions of society.

In principle, this may be a laudable aim but in practice it causes the Church to become engaged repeatedly in an undignified political struggle for control of the 'machinery' of culture. In the South, this is mainly a struggle with the departments of education and health; in the North it also leads to tension with the other Churches and with those who seek to make the Churches less tribal – for instance, the people who want Protestant and Catholic children to be educated together. I think many priests would like the Church to take on a more challenging and Christian goal.

My suggestion is that, instead of waiting for the Church to lead us in a new direction, you as ministers of the Gospel ought to take the initiative. At first you may find yourself in a very lonely place, as Jesus did. But eventually your action may lead the Church – or a significant segment of it – in a new direction. For I think we have to face the fact that the Church of the future may be much less monolithic than in the past. Whatever option you take you face a good deal of opposition. So I suggest that you don't compromise your integrity for the sake of total consensus. Don't be afraid to take a prophetic stand.

Perhaps you expect me to say you should make an option for the poor. But this phrase has become rather jaded, so I prefer to say that we need to explore how to make a *commit-*

ment to authenticity, a commitment to justice and a commitment to the Earth. Clearly this involves much more than simply importing the pastoral priorities and strategies of the more progressive sectors of the Latin American Church.

However, there is one element in common between the two situations: we have to disengage ourselves from a somewhat uncomfortable alliance with the powerful sectors of society, the ones who are profiting from the present model of development which is creating so many human and social problems and is putting the Earth itself at risk. So long as the weaker and more vulnerable groups perceive the priests to be part of the powerful 'establishment' they will feel that we are colluding in the injustices which they suffer; and this means that for them we cannot be witnesses to the Gospel. Furthermore, so long as we seek to exercise power in the conventional sense we are unable to discern how to continue Christ's mission of bringing good news to the poor and powerless.

A GOSPEL MINISTRY IN TODAY'S SOCIETY

A central aspect of the Good News brought by Jesus is that he brought meaning to people's lives by assuring them that God cares for them and is with them especially when they are troubled and disturbed. There are three ways in which ministers of the Gospel in Ireland can continue this mission of Jesus – and they offer us openings for effective contact with three different strata of society.

Firstly, we can follow Jesus in being unequivocally on

the side of those who are most 'outcast' in society; perhaps AIDS victims and the Travelling People are the equivalent today of the lepers, prostitutes and tax-collectors of the time of Jesus – not as sinners but as the outcasts of society. I would expect that all ministers of the Gospel would set this as a high priority and that some would feel called to devote themselves full-time to such ministries.

Secondly, those who wish to be authentic ministers of the Gospel can come into solidarity with the 'ordinary' poor by enabling disadvantaged individuals and groups to challenge social justice questions more effectively. The kind of activity I have in mind includes the provision of social justice advisory services; this will lead on to helping the victims of social injustice to find redress through the courts; the result, over a period of time, will be the building up of a legal framework for the protection of the weaker sections of the community. This needs to be supplemented by various other kinds of quasi-political involvement in the shaping of society – all with a view to making it more just and humane. As officially recognised ministers we can offer a great deal of help to groups organizing and campaigning for social justice (e.g., trade unions, tenants' associations, organizations for the unemployed and emigrant lobby groups). Action in pursuit of social justice on a global scale (e.g., special concern about international debt and the terms of international trade) will carry much more weight when it is linked to effective commitment to building a just society at home.

Thirdly, one of the most effective ways in which we can

be ministers of the Gospel *vis-à-vis* educated middle-class people is by being actively concerned in exploring and promoting alternatives to the present economic order which is grossly unjust and environmentally unsustainable. It is likely that one reason why 'good' middle class people in Ireland feel uneasy, rootless or alienated is that they sense that they are locked into a system that is immoral. They know they are privileged *vis-à-vis* the poorer sectors of society in this country and *vis-à-vis* the vast majority of the world's inhabitants. But they have no clear idea how that situation can be changed or what part they might play in bringing about the radical change they know is required.

They lack theoretical knowledge about possible alternatives; but the core of the difficulty is not so much lack of knowledge as the shortage of models of what a just alternative might look like in practice. Surely this is a challenge which is especially appropriate for us who feel called to be ministers of the Gospel? Working with committed lay people and members of religious communities we can help to provide the alternative models of human living of which people in this country and elsewhere are so much in need. In this way we can give people hope by showing them a foretaste of the future to which God is calling humanity and our world.

AN ALTERNATIVE APPROACH TO DEVELOPMENT

It is clear that a morally acceptable model of human development must have certain distinct qualities.

- It needs to be ecologically sustainable, so that it respects the rights of future generations to a fair share of the resources óf the earth. This means partnership with nature rather than exploitation.

- It must not promote structural unemployment or the drudgery and alienation that arises when workers have no personal involvement in the product that is produced and no say in determining the conditions of their work. There should be incentives to encourage workers to play an active part in planning their work, and to develop a friendly and supportive environment in the work-place; and this should facilitate solidarity and participative decision-making in other spheres of life, even outside the workplace.

- It must avoid the mistake of identifying 'work' with 'employment'. It seems likely that any successful future model of human development will involve having less people who are working as employees for others; instead there will be many more workers' cooperatives as well as more self-employed people.

At the heart of many of today's social problems in Ireland, North and South, lies what we may call 'The Dole Culture'. It centres around the pretence that the State can find jobs for 350,000 people and that it is trying to do so. This pretence is used as a justification for preventing people finding work on their own initiative and forcing them into the degrading dole queues. This 'Dole Culture' has all the worst features of what Pope John Paul in his recent social encyclical castigates as 'The National Assistance State'.

Jesus' parable of the eleventh hour labourer suggests that a Gospel response to unemployment is one which radically challenges the 'Dole Culture'. The worker who had to waste his day hoping for a job was treated with the same respect as the other workers; and his dignity was respected by enabling him to do some work too.

This parable does not offer us a blueprint for solving the problem of chronic unemployment; but it challenges us to find creative ways of treating all workers with dignity and allowing those who want to work to do so.

Those who wish to be ministers of the Gospel in today's world must make a serious analysis of how structural injustice operates in our particular society. This will provide a basis for avoiding collusion in injustice and for the challenge which the Gospel calls us to make to injustice in society; it should also give some indication of the kind of alternatives towards which Gospel people are called to work. We need, then, to analyze the underlying causes of today's chronic unemployment and find practical ways of escaping from the 'Dole Culture'.

It is only in the past two hundred years, with the spread of the Industrial Revolution, that most people began to depend for their living on having a 'job'. That era seems now to be drawing to a close. In future there will be less and less 'jobs' in the conventional sense. Far more people will have to earn their living by working out useful ways of working on their own initiative (as small farmers and crafts-people still do). The present jobs crisis in Ireland may be a blessing in disguise if it forces us to face up to the new situation and be 'quick off the mark' in discovering the new ways in which work will be carried out in the future.

In an appendix to this paper I shall spell out a practical proposal for eliminating the 'Dole Culture'. What I am suggesting is a course of action which is both economically and politically viable. Here it is possible only to touch on some central points. The key to it all is that instead of deliberately keeping people idle while pretending to be looking for jobs for most of the unemployed, the State should offer strong incentives to people to find or make work for themselves, subsidizing them until they reach a point where a State subsidy is no longer required.

Instead of having about 400,000 people on the dole (North and South), the State and voluntary agencies should help these people to divide themselves into two categories; Firstly, about 60,000 people in the category of 'State-assisted Job-Seekers' who will have a one in two chance of getting one of the 25,000 jobs which State and semi-state agencies can realistically hope to provide each year.

Secondly, all the remainder who will be classed as 'Subsidized Self-Employed' people. They would be paid a subsidy sufficient to enable them to live in basic dignity and would collect this in much the same way as the children's allowances. The crucial point is that they would be allowed and encouraged to earn extra money as small-time crafts-people, or by providing various services.

This approach would enable up to half a million Irish people to become free from the aimlessness and degradation of the dole queue or mindless under-paid drudgery and give them a strong incentive to explore ways of living and working effectively and humanly in the new situation which faces the world as a whole.

Need I add there will then be plenty of need and room for ministers of the Gospel to facilitate them in this search for new forms of work and a new and more human style of living.

Irish priests have enormous resources which can be devoted to the task. I don't mean money but resources of inspiration, hope, theology, and access to, and credibility with, a significant number of people who are dedicated, committed and prepared to devote their lives to what may seem to be an impossible dream.

We can give encouragement and support to two groups. On the one hand there will be those who concentrate their energy on working out ways to transform the present system from within, in a piecemeal and gradual way. On the other hand there will be those who opt out of the present system and seek to build an alternative 'from the ground up'. Both groups will need the wholehearted support from at least part of the wider community since the task is too daunting to tackle alone.

Those who dedicate themselves to this task of forming support communities of various kinds will be undertaking the modern equivalent of the founding of a religious order. In some cases, at least, the vows of poverty might be replaced by a commitment to ecological sensitivity, the vow of chastity by a commitment of fidelity to the network and the vow of obedience by a commitment to decision-making and action based on the participation of all.

By becoming involved in such committed groups each of us can find new hope in our lives – and we can help to bring the hope of Christ more effectively into our Churches and into our world.

APPENDIX: A PRACTICAL PROPOSAL ON UNEMPLOYMENT

My proposal is that we stop pretending that there is any possibility that 'jobs' can be found for the 260,000 people on the 'Live Register' in the South and 100,000 in the North. Let us instead ask the State to face up to doing two tasks both of which are economically and politically possible at present. These two tasks are:

To play a very active role in helping to provide paid employment for a limited number of people who have a realistic hope of getting a job.

To help provide a dignified and creative way of life for those who do not have paid employment, and are willing at present not to demand that the State provide them with a regular 'job'.

Within the next year our State agencies, assisted by various voluntary bodies, can help those on the 'Live Register' (plus some others who are not currently registered as 'unemployed') to sort themselves into one or other of two categories:

1. About 40,000 or 50,000 people in the South and 10,000 in the North who will be listed and helped as 'State-assisted Job-seekers'.

2. At least 250,000 people in the South and 80,000 in the North who will be listed and helped as 'Subsidized Self-employed'.

A first step is for State and semi-state agencies to draw up a realistic list of the jobs they can help to provide within the next two or three years, naming the type of work and the locality where it can be provided. At present we could expect to have about 25,000 potential jobs per year on this list in the South and, say, 5,000 in the North.

In order to be listed as a 'State-assisted Job-seeker' a person would have to be a serious applicant – qualified in terms of education, skills, personality and living location for one or other of the particular jobs that may become available. They would be paid at least £60 per week and offered free attendance at courses designed specifically to improve skills in the particular category of job for which the person is applying.

In return for the very large grants and benefits which the State gives employing companies it would have a requirement that a high proportion of the new jobs be offered first of all to those who are on the appropriate category of the list of 'State-assisted Job-seekers'. So the great advantage of being registered as a 'State-assisted Job-seeker' would be that there would be a better than two-to-one chance of actually getting one of the new jobs.

In order to keep down the numbers of people on the list of 'State-assisted Job-seekers' the State would have to make an attractive offer to many people who are currently listed as 'unemployed'. If the offer is sufficiently attractive, then many people will be willing not to go on the list of 'State-assisted Job-seekers' but to go instead on a list of 'Subsidized Self-employed Persons'. Advantages for an individual of going on to this list would be:

– They would be paid, say, £50 per week by the State.

– This money would be collected by them in much the same way as old-age pensions are handled at present, without the cost in time, money, and human dignity associated with dole queues and unemployment exchanges.

– How these people choose to spend their time would be their own affair. They would be allowed to earn extra money through providing services in various self-employed categories of work which do not qualify as regular 'paid employment'. For instance, some might set up as small-time crafts-people, others might earn some money by running a small creche or by caring for old or sick people in their homes, or by wall-papering or gardening or fixing bicycles – all on a free-enterprise basis. If any person expanded this kind of self-employment to the point where he or she earns enough to come into the tax net, then the person would be taxed like other self-employed people. In such cases the State subsidy would have to be phased out gradually, so that a 'poverty trap' would not be created.

It might be that a number of new people would wish to be registered as 'Subsidized Self-Employed Persons' – people such as housekeeping wives or husbands who do not at present have paid employment but are not on the Live Register. They would be entitled to do so, but then their spouses would be taxed at the same rate as an unmarried person (apart from allowances for children). In this way the extra cost to the State could be kept to a minimum.

In order to ensure that the list of 'State-assisted Job-seekers' does not grow too large or too small (in proportion to the potential jobs), it might be necessary to fine-tune this system by offering greater or lesser incentives to this group as compared to those on the list of 'Subsidized Self-employed Persons'. But at no point should the subsidy offered by the State to the people of either category drop below the minimum required to live with human dignity.

In this proposal I have borrowed elements from various sources and put them together in a 'package' which is simple to understand and relatively easy to implement.

Releasing Radicalism

Fintan O'Toole

Donal Door has spoken movingly and brilliantly about the idea of moral authority, about the loss of credibility which the Church has suffered among some sections of Irish society and the possibility that priests can regain that authority not because they are representatives of the Church, but in spite of that fact. Coming as I do from a secular point of view and from one suspicious of all authority that is not moral, it seems to me that he has not only spoken of this possibility but embodied it. As someone who does not wish to submit to the teaching authority of the Church, I still find what he has had to say authoritative, because it is rooted in perceptions and imbued with a spirit which I find both truthful and hopeful – a rare combination in these sometimes dark days.

I am also heartened, if somewhat flummoxed, by the fact that a section of his speech is virtually identical to a section of mine. In trying to think about what someone who can speak only, as I can, in the language of secular society, can possibly say to a group like this which is brought together and defined by a religious language, I began by sketching out the areas of what I think of as spiritual experience. None of them are specifically or necessarily religious. Yet the sense of some kind of transcendent experience in all of them is the only ground on which I can begin to feel that, if we are not talking the same language, we might still be saying some of the same things.

Those areas for me are the experiences of the transcendent which are present in sexual experience, in the experience of childbirth and parenthood, in the presence of the forces of nature, in the entering into the world of art, and in the sense of being part of a purposeful crowd. Since these are almost exactly the same areas which Donal Dorr has just listed as 'peak experiences where we find ourselves more fully human', and since this co-incidence is entirely unconscious, it may be that the task of finding a ground for dialogue is less difficult than we have come to believe.

Since I have also found from experience that there is no single group of people, nor profession in Ireland, which is in general more self-critical and more acutely aware of its own situation than the ordinary priests and nuns with whom I've come into contact in the last few years, I believe that beyond the apparent moral civil war of contemporary Ireland there are grounds for real optimism. At the very least, I believe that it is possible to find a language in which genuine dialogue, which is based neither on self-righteous liberalism nor on appeals to ancient authority, becomes possible.

It does, however, have to be stressed that not merely a language of dialogue but any kind of functionally meaningful public language is difficult in contemporary Ireland. The stress of change and the extreme openness of our societies is such that there is no given public language which can be taken for granted any more. The rhetorics of competing nationalisms, for so long the staples of public speech in Ireland, have been swept away on a tide of blood. The sense of identity that underlies meaningful public statements – the 'we' that is implied in every speech in parliament or pulpit – is under stress for the reasons that Donal Dorr has spoken about. And the increasing confusion of reality and media image which is characteristic of public life in all western countries is something we are not immune to. If you think of the way in which our public debate, in the Republic at least, has been dominated by private language, by the language of sperms and eggs and wombs and foetuses and ectopic pregnancies and the intimate troubles of marriage, for the last decade, then you get some sense of this loss of a public language. Or if you think of the serpentine confusions of the Brian Lenihan tapes affair in the presidential elections, in which not a conflict between truth and lies, but between two apparently untrue versions of the same events, was at stake, you go even further into this crisis of language.[1]

1. Since this paper was delivered, this collapse of public language has grown more obvious. In the December 1991 issue of *Studies*, Fr Patrick Reardon reflected on the question 'Can We not Discuss Morals?', taking as a starting point the incomprehension which greeted the Archbishop of Dublin Dr Connell when he called homosexuality an 'objective disorder'. In March 1992, Dr. Connell was attacked by the Labour T.D., Ruairi Quinn, for equating abortion with the Holocaust, but the Catholic Press Office denied that he had meant to do so, implying again a level of mutual incomprehensibility. And, of course, the instability and untrustworthiness of public language became most dramatically clear in the Su-

'LIBERAL' AND 'CONSERVATIVE' ...

One of the things which threatens the possibility of a functioning public language is the increasing polarisation of public life in the Republic into liberal and conservative camps, each with its own codes and meanings. These codes are becoming mutually exclusive. And, in a paradoxical way, the liberalisation of the Church after Vatican II can be said to contribute something to this process. I know that as a representative of the secular liberal media I am supposed to come here and berate you for not keeping up with the times, for not changing as society changes. That is the standard liberal charge. But, in fact, if I have anything to say it is the opposite. For it seems to me that it is precisely a crude notion of *aggiornamento* that contributes to the problem I am discussing. The idea that you as priests should tack your sails to every prevailing wind is ultimately a defeatist one. It encourages a schizophrenia in which you develop one language for dealing with the secular world, all the time keeping your own tradition in all its awkwardness behind your backs as a private tongue in which you can speak to each other but not to the public world.

There are two things about this which bother me. One is that it is precisely the awkwardness and the strangeness and the ferocity and the potential for a radicalism which is fundamentally at odds with the way the world is which is most

---

preme Court judgement in the case of *The Attorney General -v- X*. which showed the 1983 anti-abortion amendment to have virtually reversed its publicly perceived meaning in less than a decade.

---

valuable about the kind of people you are. In theory at least, you don't have a stake in things as they are. The other is that this kind of shame-faced *aggiornamento,* for all its appearance of openness, is really a defensive strategy. And it seems to me that a defensive institution is a dangerous institution. The elements of bullying and power-mongering which have been present in some aspects of the Church's public role in recent years seem to me not to be triumphalist. On the contrary, they come from a profound loss of confidence, from a sense that the barbarians are at the gate and the walls have to be re-inforced with a bitter desperation. Precisely as a secularist I believe that Irish society needs a self-confident Church, one confident enough in its own tradition to look inside it and find the radicalism that is there.

For that to be possible, though, the notion of two opposing camps of liberal and conservative Ireland must first be shown for the imprisoning fallacy it is.

For quite a long time now, we have had an easy way of explaining ourselves to ourselves, of understanding what is going on in Irish society. This paradigm has been one of conservative and liberal. Starting around 1960, the story goes, we set in motion a process of liberalisation in the Republic, a process which was, in turn, resisted by an increasingly embattled conservative majority. This story has chapters headed 'Vatican II', 'The Bishop and the Nightie', 'The Contraception Train', 'The Constitutional Crusade', 'The Abortion Referendum', 'The Divorce Referendum', 'The Case of the Virgin Condom' and so on. It is, at one level, a true story: these things have happened to us and are still happening. There is a division, or rather a series of overlapping divisions, between the Ireland of small towns and farms, of fixed property and Catholic allegiances, on the one hand, and the Ireland of fluid cities and *à la carte* menus on the other. The categories of conservatism and liberalism are a useful shorthand for these divisions.

... CATEGORIES WHIHC IMPRISON

Yet, too often, we take the shorthand for the full script and become prisoners of our own categories. So much that is sterile and wasteful about public debate in Ireland comes from the utter uselessness of those categories. For both of them are highly misleading terms.

On the one hand, when we use words like 'traditional' and 'conservative' in Ireland we are, often, dealing in imported notions that don't make much sense in relation to our specific history. Conservative societies are ones which have been able, over a long period of time, to maintain the set of ideas and values and ways of looking at the world which constitute a culture. You can be conservative if you want to maintain that culture, and the power structures which it implies, liberal or progressive if you want to modify or get rid of it. But this sort of conservatism has little place in Ireland.

We don't have a history that offers us a culture of continuity and preservation. The basic fact of our history, for at least 150 years, is that it is a history of emigration. Generation after generation has formed its children not in the values of conserving what you have in the place where you have it, but in the necessities of being elsewhere, the mechanisms of survival in a place that may well be utterly different from the one you have grown up in. We come, by and large, from a history of poverty, and the culture of poverty is a culture of adapting to survive, not of conservative clinging to fixed points on the historical or geographical compass. A poor conservative is a dead conservative. We have to change in order to live.

It is true that Irish people throughout the generations have clung to loyalties of religion and nationality and family, but clung as a man shipwrecked in a violent sea clings to a fragment of his shattered boat, not as the inhabitant of a stable, ordered society clings to an established hierarchy of values. We held on to certain things to allow us to cope with change, not to help us to avoid it.

It is this peculiar sense of tradition or conservatism which has been evident in the recent struggles of Irish public life. The people I met campaigning for the anti-abortion amendment or the divorce referendum from a right-wing Catholic perspective, the people I talked to at a moving statue, the people you still see campaigning against condoms or the decriminalisation of homosexuality, are not the serene, self-confident inheritors of a long tradition. They are the hurt, bewildered, often embittered inheritors of a sense of fracture and alienation. For conservatives, they tend to be a pretty radical, disaffected and angry bunch of people, no more a part of the political mainstream than people on the far left of politics would be.

On the other hand, the word 'liberal' is no more precise or accurate. 'Liberal', notoriously, has two different and at times contradictory meanings. In the sense in which it is used in American politics, it is an indicator of a progressive, enlightened attitude which supports the notion of an interventionist and welfare-oriented state. In the sense in which it is used in relation to economics in Britain and elsewhere, it has an almost precisely opposite meaning: the free-market, *laissez-faire*, deregulation, the disparagement, in Mrs Thatcher's words of 'people drooling and dribbling about compassion'.

And in the Irish context, it is possible, particularly for a large section of the urban middle-class, to combine aspects of these two meanings, to be 'progressive' on issues of private morality and the separation of Church and State, and yet quite contented with the economic *status quo*. This linguistic confusion reaches its height in the way in which we use the phrase 'social issues' in Ireland to mean its exact opposite: issues of private conscience, private morality, private behaviour. It is also part of the fatal ambiguity present in the idea of tolerance.

To be tolerant is to accept the presence in your society of Protestants, atheists, divorcees, teenage sex, homosexuals, and so on. But it is also to accept and tolerate unemployment, emigration, poverty, and the bankruptcy of the political system. One side of the coin is conducive to a better sort of society. The other isn't. But both can co-exist within the comfort of the term 'liberal'.

The liberal/conservative paradigm survives because it is mutually self-justifying. As a liberal, I can refuse to think about the failure of public and social values in my society and still feel, because I have the right line on individual conscience, that I am a good citizen. As a conservative, I can fight the good fight without questioning the power structures of my society and still feel that I am being not only a good citizen but a good Catholic. By fighting the alien horde of corrupters, I don't have to think about any of the radical and difficult visions of social solidarity and individual dignity which are inherent in my faith. Each of us, the liberal and the conservative, is validated by the presence of the other.

There are dozens of ways in which this self-justifying use of categories serves to obscure rather than to illuminate the society in which we live. To take just one of them, the notion of family which has been a constant in recent Irish political debate, is one which often denied any meaning by the lines on which it is discussed. To the liberals, family is a conservative weapon, a code *they* use to get at *us*. To the conservatives, who are often genuinely and deeply concerned about the threat to family life in modern society, the insistence on seeing these threats as being about the erosion of abstract values and not about real things happening to real people – emigration, the workaholic ethic, the abuse of children – renders impotent and incoherent the critique which has to be made. One side doesn't want to talk about the family, the other side doesn't want to talk about the things that really threaten it (as opposed to the things which a set of dogmas says must threaten it). The result is that, far from there being a clear and passionate debate along entrenched lines, there is really no debate at all.

THE RADICAL HEART OF FAITH

The continuing insistence on seeing our situation in terms of liberal versus conservative is particularly disabling for many people within the Catholic Church. Because the paradigm constantly seems to put them in the conservative camp, they are often unable to realise the potential for radical and unsettling disturbance which is at the heart of their faith. Defensive and mesmerised by the demand that they ought to accommodate themselves to liberalism, they fail to notice that this demand is itself a fundamentally conservative one, assuming as it does that the way things are is the way they ought to be.

There are, I know, many of you who are already leaving these sterile oppositions behind. The most powerful and challenging things that are happening in the Church are not the attempts to alter the message to suit the times, but the determination of those who are confident of the richness of their own tradition to unleash the critical powers that are at its heart. Many of you find in the Gospels not a confirmation of the way things are now but a call to arms in the cause of a different sort of society. I hope and believe that that call will find an echo beyond the boundaries of your own tradition.

Resolutions Passed at the 1991 AGM of the NCPI

1. Where a priest chooses not to be chairperson of the school management board, he should not be asked to do so.

2. That the possibility and feasibility of employing lay people for full-time pastoral ministry in the Church be investigated.

3. That this conference recognises the parish structure, as a model of gathering that gives life and meaning to people, to be a model experiencing crisis. It is an urgent task of evangelization to explore new models of gathering which are life-giving and meaningful. Therefore we call on the Executive to address this issue as a priority.

4. NCPI asks that bishops ensure that the first appointment of newly ordained priests would be to a ministry in which they would be working with other priests.

5. That the Executive of NCPI explore, through its members and with the bishops, the CMRS and the IMU, ways of promoting the NCPI renewal courses and other renewal facilities.

The Ryan Report on Renewal Courses for Priests

At a meeting in April, 1990, the national executive of the NCPI decided to set up a special committee to review renewal courses for priests and to suggest emendations and ways forward.

The committee members were: Bishop Laurence Ryan (Chairperson), Fr Eamon Bredin, Mrs Anne Cantwell, Fr Jim Cassin, Fr Pat Collins, Mr Tom Collins, Sr Sylvia Diamond, O.P., Mrs Mary Howlett, Fr Joe MacMahon, Fr Ciary Quirke.

The committee held a two-day seminar on the renewal of priests to which representatives of priests' councils, people involved in running renewal courses and other interested persons were invited. Over thirty people attended. Out of this seminar came a report which the committee subsequently came to regard as a foundational document for its own reflections and discussions.

The final report is given here. It is called the Ryan Report after the chairperson of the committee, Dr Laurence Ryan, Bishop of Kildare and Leighlin.

FINDINGS

1.1 Introduction

During the course of our investigations and discussions, we have become aware of the many efforts being made at national and local levels to advance the renewal of the Church in Ireland. We have been encouraged by these initiatives and the help they have been to individual priests and to the Church at large. We wish to place on record our acknowledgement of and full support for the many positive things taking place in the Irish Church at different levels, particularly in the area of our interest – the renewal of priests. The suggestions made in this report should be understood as complementing the efforts already being made to advance renewal.

We have also become more conscious of the enormous and increasing diversity of opinions, values, attitudes and priorities in society and in the Church in Ireland. Change and diversity have always been part of the human story but what is different now is the pace of change and the extent of diversity and the certainty that these are accelerating and broadening.

Since Vatican II we have become aware of different models of understanding the Church and different ways of ministering. No longer is it possible to speak of a single vision of Church but of a variety of visions, of a monolithic model of priest but of different models. Trying to make sense of this enormous diversity is becoming increasingly more difficult. Yet this is the task facing the priest in the 1990s.

1.2 How Can the Priest Be Helped to Cope?

We believe, and we hold this as a fundamental principle, that the renewal of the priest is only one element in a multidimensional approach to renewal in the Church. Attempts at renewal of priests are doomed to failure if they happen, and are seen to happen, in isolation from the wider renewal in each local Church – in parishes, religious communities and organisations and among individuals. All the strands of renewal have to go hand-in-hand.

1.3 Our Analysis of the Situation

The Committee spent much time deliberating on the report from the seminar on 'Renewal of Priests in Ireland' in an attempt to understand what it was saying to us about what priests are looking for explicitly and more especially implicitly. What we were searching for, in other words, was some kind of profile of the priest in Ireland in the 1990s out of which would emerge a programme of renewal or at least would indicate the direction such a programme should take.

Analysing the document we found that, although it addresses the narrower issue of renewal courses for priests, it contains

a) a lot of material touching on the perceived personal and interpersonal needs of the priests;

b) a number of pointers to issues and concerns of a systemic nature which priests are grappling with; by *systemic* we mean the sum total of the connected parts making up the body – in this case the Church – and how they inter-relate.

It is also evident from the report that by and large renewal courses, including the NCPI course, respond satisfactorily to the perceived personal and interpersonal needs of the priest but not to the wider systemic issues. Running through the document is a tension between the remedial or therapeutic dimension of renewal courses, which is found to be beneficial, and their failure to help the priest respond to the total environment or system to which he must return at the end of the course, an environment which is intractable at best and hostile at worst. Throughout the report there is a despair about changing the system.

We have come to the conclusion that if we were to suggest a continuation of existing renewal courses without addressing the systemic issues, we could well be accused of merely providing a short-term survival-kit for the priest, while in the longer term reinforcing the *status quo* and declaring implicitly that the system cannot be changed. We believe that the system can be changed. This raises the question:

What are renewal courses for?

Are they naive about change, systems and the nature of renewal itself?

Are they merely a short-term survival-kit for the priest?

There is not doubt that courses are necessary to deal with personal needs and we readily recognise and acknowledge their contribution in this area, but meeting these needs cannot be an end in itself. Unless the wider renewal is undertaken and the whole systemic issue is addressed, courses will be largely counter-productive and will eventually lead participants to experience greater frustration. A new approach is needed so that priests coming off course are not doomed to muddle along in the present system. The fruitfulness of renewal courses will continue to be limited until the wider renewal of the component parts of the system is undertaken.

1.4 The Systemic Approach

The new approach will have to look at the system and the visions or philosophy that inspire them, at the notion of change and how systems are changed. Taking the diocese as a total system and each parish as a subsystem, a number of basic questions have to be asked and answers given:

> What are the principal inspirational visions currently prevailing in the diocese?
>
> What are the structures that incarnate these visions?
>
> Do the visions and their structures lead to a flourishing of humans or to their withering?
>
> How do these visions correspond with the guiding principles of Vatican II.

But asking and answering these questions and devoting a significant amount of time to examining systemic change in renewal courses are not enough in themselves. For genuine renewal to take place, the following requirements are essential:

> The whole diocese must be committed to real change by challenging the visions prevailing in the diocese with the guiding principles of Vatican II.
>
> All in the diocese have a responsibility to facilitate this change, especially those who have been exposed to renewal courses.

If these requirements are missing, then no matter how many priests follow courses, little will change. But once the commitments are given, then the nature of change within the system and the subsystems can be addressed and eventually the necessary structures put in place.

Implementing this new approach obviously involves far more than a restructuring of existing courses so as to make room for the systemic dimension. The aim of renewal is to enable all members of the local Church, clergy, laity and religious, to grow together in Christian fellowship and apostolic responsibility at the service of God's Kingdom. This involves ministering collaboratively.

For they [pastors] know that they themselves were not established by Christ to undertake alone the whole salvific mission of the Church to the world, but that it is their exalted office so to be shepherds of the faithful and also recognise the latter's contribution and charisms that everyone in his own way will, with one mind, co-operate in the common task.(*Lumen Gentium*, 30)

One of the major challenges facing bishops, priests and religious is to accept that all Christians are called to ministry and that, therefore, they must learn to let go so that others can assume their responsibility by sharing in the ministry of the Church. The renewal of the local Church must be undertaken by all who make up the Church. This is multi-faceted operation which has to respect the diversity of charisms. Renewal should not be understood as an attempt to brainwash people to follow one official line or vision nor regiment them within fixed and rigid structures. All should be able to feel that their story is listened to, their gifts recognised and utilised and their views respected.

Letting go on the part of the clergy and ministering in a collaborative way will be painful but beneficial because it will allow the priest to lessen his sense of loneliness, let go of the burden of having to be 'able for everything' and demolish the accusations of being irrelevant and inefficient. Collaborating with others will make the priest more whole as a person and as a minister.

RECOMMENDATIONS

2.1 We take it as a fundamental principle that conversion and renewal are essential elements of Christian life at personal, community and institutional levels. The call to conversion and renewal involves for the priest, among other things, a willingness to undertake 'cultural and spiritual updating', in the words of Pope John Paul II. Because of its enormous implications, all the necessary resources – personnel and financial – should be made available to carry out the renewal required at all levels.

Since renewal of the Church is a multidimensional reality, we intend to make recommendations relating to different levels of Church life before going on to make specific suggestions regarding renewal courses for priests.

It may seem unrealistic to be putting forward suggestions for action to a body about matters over which it has little control, but the NCPI has expressed its desire and willingness to promote renewal in the Church, especially as it touches on the lives of priests. Therefore, the NCPI may be able to encourage and initiate dialogue and promote efforts to bring about changes along the lines suggested in this report. In fact, we believe that the NCPI representatives in each diocese have a special responsibility to bring to the attention of their bishops and fellow-priests the import and recommendations of this report.

Recommendations relating to the wider renewal are continued in PART ONE, while PART TWO contains proposals relating specifically to renewal courses.

PART ONE

3.1 Diocesan Level

i) Both as a measure of their commitment to, and as a pre-requisite for change, bishops should be willing to take courses so that they can better understand the systemic approach as well as acquire the necessary personal skills in leadership. A collaborative, supportive and challenging style of leadership is needed at this time.

ii) Diocesan assemblies and other diocesan structures for communication and collaboration may need to be subjected to a critical evaluation of their past performance with a view to improving their effectiveness. The feeling among priests is that by and large assemblies have been ineffective and that their potential has been untapped.

iii) Structures for dialogue between bishops, parish priests, curates, laity and religious need to be set up in order to improve communication and increase awareness of their common mission and each one's specific role. However, there is need to go beyond dialogue to the setting up of structures for collaborative ministry.

iv) Support for priests should be tailored according to their needs. Therefore, we strongly recommend a post-ordination programme for newly ordained priests along the lines of programmes operating in the U.S.A. and elsewhere. Through accompaniment and a process of reflection on his experiences, such a programme would provide support and affirmation and help the young priest develop the skills needed to meet the challenges of the active ministry.

v) Decision-makers, especially parish priests – already in position or about to be appointed – should be invited as part of their preparation for the job, to do a renewal course.

vi) Each diocese should have a committee with responsibility for organising and supervising a wide variety of programmes of ongoing formation for clergy and laity. This committee should include some lay members.

3.2 Parish Level

Attempts at various degrees of collaborative ministry have been successfully tried in parishes around the country. The NCPI will help promote renewal by publicising these efforts among the membership so that other priests will be encouraged to undertake similar projects in their own parishes. What we have in mind here is that the NCPI would be a resource group spreading ideas and information on successful projects.

3.3 Individual Level

i) As a general rule, priests should regard it as a desirable and

---

119

normal part of their lives to take a sabbatical break every seven years as the term suggests. Also there are particular moments or landmarks when ongoing formation will be appropriate:

> at least within ten years of ordination
> on the occasion of the silver jubilee of ordination
> as preparation for a new ministry
> at a time of severe crisis
> as preparation for retirement.

ii) We believe that various forms of priestly fellowship or support groups should be encouraged and promoted. Not only is this beneficial as a source of support but it can serve as an instrument for ongoing formation.

3.4 Seminaries

Although our brief did not include looking at seminary formation, it became very clear to us that formation in the seminaries is an integral part of both the wider renewal int eh Church and the particular renewal of the individual priest so that what we have been saying in this report has major implications for seminaries.

PART TWO

4.1 Renewal Courses

The recommendations outlined in this part refer to all renewal courses for priests but have special reference to the NCPI course.

As we have stated above, the present NCPI course serves a very useful purpose in meeting some of the personal and interpersonal needs of priests to a satisfactory degree. However, it does not address the systemic issues. In order to redress this lack, a new module should be introduced into the course which would deal with

- systems and the visions that inspire them
- the structures that incarnate the visions
- change and how systems can be changed
- priesthood: what is a priest for? the role and the person

- models of ministry: the interpersonal versus the collaborative or systemic
- skills for letting go and sharing responsibility

This module should be introduced at the beginning of the course so that participants can begin to cope with the notion of change and understand the course as part of a multi-faceted approach to renewal. It is also important that the course equip priests with the tools they need to implement back home what they have experienced and learned on the course.

4.2 Ongoing Support

One of the major problems facing priests coming off courses is the lack of structures and a supportive environment back home. What we are saying is that the NCPI should pay special attention to the follow-up of courses by setting up structures which will enable priests to implement what they have absorbed from the course and to deal with personal issues that may have arisen since the course. The need for such structures is one of the loudest cries for help coming out of the All Hallows report.

As a follow-up to existing courses, we therefore recommend the following steps.

i) Upon completion of the course, and in collaboration with the diocese, each participant should be given a project on collaborative ministry to be put into operation within a certain time back home. This will be assessed by the course director or others appointed by him. Such a project would ensure that what has been learned on the course would be put into practice within the context of, and with the active support and co-operation of the diocese.

ii) We urge that an effort be made to ensure that a large group of priests from the same diocese or all the priests from two or three adjoining parishes or even all from the one parish do the renewal course together so that they can form a nucleus for continuing renewal within the diocese. It is essential however, that they set up support groups (not exclusively clerical) so that the momentum for renewal can be kept going. What happens after the course is often more important than what takes place at it.

iii) We welcome the increased emphasis being placed in the NCPI course on the spiritual development of the priest. The NCPI should further this by publishing the names and addresses of spiritual directors around the country who would be willing and available to provide this service.

4.3 New Types of Courses

i) Ideally, renewal courses for priests should include laity and religious with a good representation of women so as to bring to the courses a richer dimension than is provided at present. We realise that this is not always easy, given the fact that most laity cannot take time off for the longer course due to various factors. Mixed renewal courses do not exclude the need for shorter courses for priests alone who, like any other group, need space for themselves.

ii) Shorter courses for priests, laity and religious should be organised at diocesan and parish level by the diocesan committee for on-going formation.

iii) The NCPI could usefully sponsor short courses (day-long, weekend) on collaborative ministry to which priests could bring along five or six laity from their parishes or places of work.